KNew Me

KNew Me

---

10 MEN . 10 STORIES
of Perseverance

CO-AUTHORS:

DR. JOSEPH ACQUAYE . RANDELL ADJEI

NICHOLAS BARHAM . JAMAL CAMPBELL . JELANI DANIEL

CHRIS DUFF . KEITH HILL JR. . JEFF A.D. MARTIN

JERMAINE SPENCE . DANNY STONE

Facebook:

KNew Me Movement

INSTAGRAM:

@KNew.Me.Movement

Cover design and book layout by:

 Mark Anthoney Blackwood

www.markanthoney.com

Edited by:

Line4Line Editing & Proofreading

Printed in Canada

First Printing, August 2019

ISBN 978-1-9995769-3-6

J. A. D. M. Consulting

Dedication:

This book is dedicated to all men both young and old, who are simply striving to become the best version of themselves each and every day.

CONTENTS

INTRODUCTION

This book was created for the everyday man. The man who despite trying to do his best, sometimes simply falls short. For the man who can sometimes become lost in the world trying to figure out who he truly is. For the man who to his core simply wants to do right by his children, his spouse, his girlfriend, his family and his community; but stumbles along his journey. For the man who wears the disguise of masculinity in efforts to live up to the standards laid out through societal norms, but behind that disguise, he hides the fact that he is vulnerable, he is fearful, he has self-doubt and he is in search of identity. For the everyday male lost in the struggle and believes that he suffers alone...This book is specifically compiled and written for you.

The goal of this book is not to entertain you with stories of obstacles faced by the various male authors. The objective is to show you that ordinary men, just like you have gone through hardships, have faced dismal circumstances and have been lost in many aspects along their own way. They were able to clean up their mess, stand on top of their tribulation and become better men because of it. The men who wrote this book are not super heroes by any stretch of the term. They are simply men, who understand what it means to struggle, what it means to assimilate into a societal definition of manhood and what it means to suppress vulnerability to conceal fear and to hide self-doubt. Men who know what it feels like to screw up but believe that telling their truth will help others who might be travelling through a similar journey. Men who care enough to see you win!

In helping to deliver this message of triumph, I reached out to men who are trailblazers and leaders within their own right. Men of service who have and continue to put the needs of others in front of their own; not because they are paid or made to do so, but because they believe they were called to do so. Although these men have the same common goal of helping people become the best version of themselves, they all found their own unique way of achieving this. The co-writers of this book range from life coaches, youth workers, motivational speakers, entrepreneurs, authors, doctors, teachers, community leaders and mentors; all positions that start by putting the needs of others in front of their own.

Bringing together men who are leaders within their own field was important. Even more imperative than that, I needed to choose men who not only have fallen along the journey of life, but despite the cuts and bruising from that plunge, they still had the burning desire, passion and determination to stand back up. Men who have faced hardships, who have been through the storm and who are not afraid to share their story. Men who can speak about their struggles because they are brave enough, men who can teach from a level of experience because they have lived enough and men who can admit to their mistakes because they are open and honest enough. I wanted to ensure that each man contributing to this book could unequivocally stand as an example for any young man who is starting his journey. For any gentleman who is going through a struggle, for any guy who has gotten lost along his way and for anyone who needs to hear stories of triumph to propel them forward. In their own personal chapters, these men speak about their life journey and some of the obstacles they faced. Some of the stories may resonate with you more than others, as you may see a reflection of your own narrative within them. As personal as every story is to the writer, your path is just as particular to you. However, even if your life's journey is not in any way comparable, what is relatable on the most basic of human levels is learning to step through your adversity. That is the exact premise of this book. To push you through your most difficult struggles and find the best version of yourself on the other side. These men do the work that they do, because they were called to serve. They co-authored this book, because they were called to serve and they open up about their lives because again, they were called to serve. As a collective, these co-authors all believe that if they can help someone to become a better father, to become a loyal husband, to become an upstanding mentor, to be a giver, to show love, to step through barriers, to inspire, to beat addiction, to own their greatness, to find spirituality or to break generational cycles, then any exposed vulnerability, embarrassment or openness that they bare in their stories is all completely worth it!

What is important for you to follow is the lessons at the end of every chapter. Each author pulls out the main lessons they learned within their story in order for you to use as a reference to go back to time and time again and apply to your own life. Every story may not be totally relatable to you, but the lessons can be applied to every aspect within your life.

The title of this book KNew Me has a double meaning. Knew me, is in reference to the bible verse found in Jeremiah 1:5, "Before I formed you in the womb I knew you, before you were born I set you apart…" What this signifies is that before you were born, before you were an embryo, before you were even a thought in your parent's mind, God recognized you. Because you were distinguished, even before your little heart could palpitate, you as a specific individual, the only YOU to ever walk this earth, the only you to have your own singular set of DNA and fingerprints in the history of life are identified and your life has supreme significance! Understand how valuable your life is! Your life absolutely matters! Once you can truly comprehend that you are rare, a one of a kind work of art, you will start to understand and appreciate your worth and recognize the importance of letting your old self depart.

The second meaning to the title is exactly that, dying of the old, to create a New me. Once and for all, doing away with that long-lasting anger and bitterness. Learning to step through fear and control self-doubt or any other emotion that has been holding you back. Being able to step into a world where your mission is to be a better man in all facets and in every area of your life. Yes, you will have setbacks. Indeed, you will suffer failures and of course, you will encounter negative influences, but learning not to hold onto them will create the new you that will catapult you into your purpose.

A powerful and resonating quote from James Allen's classic self-help book, As A Man Thinketh says that, "a man cannot directly choose his circumstances, but he can choose his thoughts and so indirectly, yet surely, shape his circumstances." The men of this book are here to open up your thoughts so you can reshape your circumstance for the better. No more will you need to live with the pressures of feeling that you aren't enough, that you're inadequate for your children, that you fall short with your significant other, that you're deficient in the relationships in your life or that you lack the tools to become who you truly want to be. This is the day when YOU start reshaping your thinking and realize that everything you've ever needed is already inside of you, but it does start by reshaping your thoughts.

As human beings, we are going to have setbacks in our lives, but understand that the pitfalls along your path do not define you! Be encouraged. Don't give up and know that whatever problem you might be facing, you WILL make it through. My men, my fellas, my brothers here is to creating and maintaining the best version of you there will ever be!
KNew Me!

Jeff A.D. Martin

CHAPTER ONE

SHOW ME YOUR FRIENDS

By Danny Stone

"Show me your friends and I will tell you who you are."

Monica Stone (my grandmother)

Life is an interesting journey full of twists and turns, ups and downs, clarity and uncertainty. Just when you seem to be making progress in your career, relationship, finances, health or as a parent, something jumps up and knocks you down. Not all the time, just at the most inconvenient times. The question is how do you get back up? How do you continue to fight to live your best life when you have so many obstacles in your way? Some would say you just have to get up and get going but that is easier said than done. If you don`t have the confidence and lack the vision to see something greater for yourself it is difficult to get back on track. I know; I have been knocked down and felt lost many times in my life. I have strived towards becoming the best version of myself, living the life I want and I have had setbacks along the way. Many times I had to figure out how to get up and continue on my journey. Maybe you can relate, maybe you are going through something right now and you are struggling to find yourself. Struggling to move forward or to get back to your confident self.

It's been a long journey to get to this point in my life; it was a long road to go from growing up poor in low-income housing to an author, speaker and success coach that travels the world. I've gotten to this point by having mentors, taking time to understand myself and dreaming big. One of my biggest mentors was my grandmother. She passed away from cancer in 2005, but she left me with so many life lessons; lessons that helped to shape who I am today.

Show me your friends and I will tell you who you are, is one of the things my Jamaican grandmother used to say to me often growing up. Of course, I never knew what it meant when I was younger, but I knew it had to be important because it is one of the things she always said to me. It wasn't until much later in life that I understood what it meant and why it was so important for me to understand. Once I understood what she was trying to tell me, it changed my life forever and helped me to become the driver of my life.

Let me take you back to my childhood for you to truly understand how I went from growing up in a low-income housing project headed for a life of crime, to an entrepreneur doing what I love and travelling the world.

Growing up in the inner city surrounded by drugs, crime and violence I didn't know who I was. Every day I would see older guys and "friends" selling drugs on the corner and it was often to people we knew. There were thefts, robberies, violence and unfortunately murders in my community. I was lost and didn't know who I was or whom I wanted to be. I got bullied and picked on by other kids in my neighborhood because I didn't have name brand clothes or I just happened to be the target for the day. I didn't have any positive male role models at the time (so I thought) so naturally, like so many other young Black men in poor communities, I got caught up in a life of crime. It was easy to become a follower because I was lost. I needed acceptance, I wanted to fit in and I didn't want to be an outcast. Like many other young people, I wanted to be liked and cool and I was constantly seeking approval from others.

I had no hope or goals because I never thought that far ahead. Many of my friends were the same. We lived day by day and many of us never expected to live past the age of 21. The saying by many people who grow up in similar environments is true for me. You may have heard people say I was either going to end up in jail or dead. That was my reality growing up in my neighborhood. I had friends that had been killed and even more that had been in and out of jail for selling drugs, murder and other crimes. To be really honest, as smart as I knew I was and as different as I knew I was, deep down I thought this was going to be my reality. I really thought I would end up in jail or possibly, dead for the lifestyle I was living and the people

I was hanging around with. I used to count problems instead of counting blessings. I would focus on what I didn't have: my father wasn't around, my clothes were not name-brand and there were times that our family struggled to pay the bills. My focus was on what was going wrong, which allowed me to justify why I was doing wrong in my life. Having a negative mindset attracted more negativity in my life, it attracted more challenges and I developed a passenger's mindset. What I mean by this is that when you are a passenger in life, you let life happen. You have no goals or dreams. The bar is set very low so you don't disappoint yourself by not getting what you want.

If you are a passenger you let other people's opinion guide your decisions, you let your environment tell you who you are and you don't believe in your potential.

I was a passenger in my own life. My friends and my environment told me who I was and I sat back and believed it. I believed that I couldn't do more with my life and I hung around people who had no plans to do anything else other than to live a mediocre existence.

I'm not saying my childhood and teenage years were all bad, I had many great moments. I had a loving family, we were very close. We often had family cookouts and gatherings, I got to be outdoors at the beach or on the lake and spent hours on the basketball court with friends. I was a pretty good athlete and I sometimes had articles written about me In the local newspaper highlighting my basketball skills in junior high school and high school. Of course, my life was not all bad, just like I am sure your life is not all bad. It is about having a balance of amazing experiences and challenges. The difference is all about what you focus on the most and what you believe is possible for you in your life. There were times that I knew I would get out of my neighbourhood and live a better life but there were times I didn't think I would ever leave. For the most part, I lived day by day and set the bar low because I was afraid of failure and I was afraid of success. I was concerned about what others would say. I was afraid they wouldn't like me or they would ridicule me for wanting something different than they wanted. I wanted more out of life I just didn't know what I really wanted. I was fortunate enough to have mentors along the way; my grandmother, uncles and basketball coaches who all encouraged me that I could do more with my life. I just couldn't see it for myself. I was lost and needed to be found.

One day all of that changed. It was the day that my life shifted forever, the day that was the beginning of my journey to find my purpose and greatness. It was the day I understood that message my grandmother had told me all of my life. I was 18 years old. I had already been arrested for stealing cars and other small crimes, fortunately for me I was given a second chance by the courts. If I stayed out of trouble while I was on probation, all charges would be removed from my record and that's exactly what I did.

I had to start thinking about what I was going to do after high school. My mother and grandmother had been telling me that I needed to apply to universities, but I wasn't sure I wanted to go. I was getting letters from university basketball coaches trying to recruit me to their schools to play and the pressure was on me to make a decision. It was a decision that I struggled with. I didn't know if I wanted to leave my neighbourhood and leave my friends and I didn't think I was smart enough to go to university.

It was a hot sunny day, I was sitting outside with some friends in the parking lot drinking alcohol, some of my friends were smoking marijuana and others were selling drugs. As I sat there something came over me. I looked around at my friends and I thought about my other friends that had been in jail and the ones that got killed. It hit me; my grandmother's saying finally rang true to me. I was who I associated with. I was someone who was a passenger in my own life. I let life happen to me. I had no goals, no hopes, no dreams and I was simply following the path my friends had forged.

CHAPTER ONE

I thought about going to university, about getting out of the neighbourhood and about changing my life for the better. As I sat there with my friends, I knew this was the time to tell them something really important. I knew it would change our relationships and I suspected things would be different, but I had to say what was on my mind. I was nervous, scared, my hands were clammy. My heart was beating fast and I was sweating, I knew this was the time to speak up, even though I wasn't really ready. I said to them, "Yo, I think I'm going to play ball in university, you know rep our hood too," they all just looked at me and one of my friends said, "What? You are trying to go to school?" I said, "Yes, I want to go to school and play basketball and probably get a degree." Immediately they all laughed and told me it was stupid. They said making money was the most important thing, how being in the streets and making money was all they cared about. They said that school was a waste of time and no one had time for that, they called me more names and used a bunch of expletives. Then they all got up and left me sitting there alone. I sat there with mixed emotions; I was sad and wanted to cry but I was angry that they called me names and left, ultimately I just felt alone.

It was in this moment that I woke up and knew that they weren't really my friends and I wanted more out of life. I went from being a passenger to being the driver of my life. I was taking control of what was best for me and not letting other people tell me or encourage me to do what they wanted me to do. I knew that things would be different from that moment on. That one decision and conversation changed my life forever. That summer almost all of my friends stopped talking to me. They treated me like an outsider in my own community. They laughed at me and picked on me because I decided I was going to university. Even though it was difficult I accepted it, I went on to attend university and played basketball. I received the Rookie of the Year my first year playing and Outstanding Player of the Year my second year from my men's university basketball team. I got an education and moved on to become a Youth Outreach Worker working with many of the youth that lived in my old community and other low-income communities. Then later I managed training for major companies until I started my own business and became an author, speaker, coach and personal development teacher helping people change their lives. It started with that one seed planted by my grandmother and nurtured by my family members, mentors and others. I learned many lessons that day. I learned that you have to walk your own path. You have to be the driver of your life. It doesn't matter what others have to say, it doesn't matter what your circumstances are, where you grew up or the challenges that you have had; you are the one who has the ability to change your life. The other lesson that I learned is that you are who you associate with the most. That is what my grandmother tried to explain to me many times. The people that you hang around most are a reflection of who you are or who you will become. If you hang around negative people, you will become a negative person. If you hang around positive people, you will become a positive person. If you hang around criminals, you ARE a criminal. If you spend most of your time with people who are moving forward in life and have big goals then you will be the same. I got it. The third thing I learned that day is to be careful who you tell your goals and dreams to. I learned that not everyone wants to see you win. Not everyone will believe in your goals and dreams and often they will discourage you from pursuing them. It is difficult for someone to see your vision for your life because they cannot see bigger things in their own life. It's difficult for someone who isn't happy in their job or relationship to be happy that you are pursuing your passion or that you are in a loving relationship. I learned to be selective about who I tell my goals and dreams to. I only share my ambitions with people that are supportive, positive and hold me accountable.

Since making that decision at the age of 18, I have had many other challenges in my life and I have had to make many other decisions that affected my journey. I have had to make difficult decisions about my career, my relationships, about my friends and about deciding what I wanted in my life. My journey has been full of roadblocks, challenges and disappointment just like most people, but I am still here. I'm still moving forward and I'm still on my journey to becoming the person that I want to be and live the life that I want to live.

I share this with you because maybe you can relate to this. Maybe you are feeling stuck in your life or you want more and don't know how to move forward. Maybe the people around you are stuck too and cannot show you the way out. Maybe they are very negative and often shoot down your goals and dreams. It's possible that you are a passenger in your own life, letting life happen and going through the motions of your daily routines. You may be working in a job that is unfulfilling, stressful and you are feeling overworked and unappreciated. Perhaps like me in the past, you are in a relationship with someone that doesn't treat you like you deserve to be treated or with someone who is not supportive of your dreams. You need to know that you can be the driver of your life. You can choose to get out of the passenger's seat and get into the driver's seat. You can take control of your life and change whatever is not working or holding you back from living the life you want and becoming the person you want to be. The minute you decide that you have greatness within you and that you can achieve amazing things in your life a shift will happen within you. Once that shift happens and you commit to doing something about it and take massive action, daily action, your life will change. The most incredible thing about making the decision to become the driver of your life is that you can shift from a passenger mindset to a driver mindset anytime you choose. You are NEVER locked into the passenger seat of your life. You always have the opportunity to strive towards greatness and live up to your potential.

To this day I am very selective about whom I spend most of my time with and I connect with positive, powerful, goal-getters (people who chase big goals). Are you a goal-getter? Do you have big goals that you want to achieve? Are you taking consistent, daily action or do you do something towards your goals occasionally? Do you count your blessings or do you count your problems? What type of self-talk do you have going on in your mind? Is it positive self-talk or are you negative? Do you have mentors, coaches, friends or family members that encourage you, teach you and hold you accountable?

You are always going to have challenges in life. People are often going to doubt your decisions and be unsupportive of your quest for greatness. They won't understand your vision for your life and why you make some of the decisions that you make to move your life forward. That's fine, it's your life. No one can understand your vision, your goals, your desire to find your true purpose and serve others because it is not their journey, it's YOURS! Never be afraid to put yourself and your needs first because you matter. Your goals and dreams matter. Your desire to seek out your greatness matters. You need to remind yourself of this daily. You need to look in the mirror and tell yourself that you have greatness within and you deserve to be the best version of yourself. You own your happiness. You own your success. Your story is yours to tell and the ending is yours to change. You don't have to believe in yourself fully before you take action, you can take action until you begin to believe in yourself and use that as fire to keep you going.

I had people doubt me when I left a "good" job in the corporate world to follow my passion of helping others find theirs. I doubted myself, I wasn't sure I was ready, but I had great mentors that encouraged me to make the leap, so I did and it's been an amazing journey. People doubted me when I told them that I was writing a book, I didn't know how to write a book, but I knew I had a message to get out to the world, so I wrote You Have the Keys, Now Drive. The book has sold thousands of copies and reached readers in seven countries so far. People are always going to doubt you, you are going to doubt yourself at times, there will be times that you struggle to find a way to make your dreams happen, but you must keep going. Always move forward, take one step at a time, one day at a time, connect with the right people, develop a plan and wake up every day and do the most important things that will get you closer to where you want to be in your life. Continue to raise the bar, set bigger goals and take massive action and you will tap into your best version of yourself.

I have to bring this story full circle. It was nineteen years after I had that life changing conversation with my friends at the age of 18. The conversation where my friends laughed at me and ridiculed me for wanting to do something positive with my life instead of living a life of crime. One day I logged into my social media account and I saw a message from one of the main guys who degraded me that day, he was one of the ring leaders that encouraged everyone to stop associating with me. In his message he said that he had been in and out of jail for the past 12 years and since coming out he changed his life. He told me he had been watching my posts on social media and he was proud of the person I had become. He said that I made the right choice to go my own way many years ago and that he admired me and the work that I was doing. "I always knew that you would do big things," he said in his message. I acknowledged him and told him I appreciated his message and to keep on his positive path. We still continue to speak to this day and he continues his journey to become a better version of himself. His life has completely changed, he is in a long-term relationship and he now owns his own carpentry company and has a few employees who work with him on various contracts. What I realized is that people who feel stuck, trapped and lost often don't know how to move forward. When or if they see someone taking action to achieve their goals it becomes a reality check for them and it is often one that they are not ready for so they lash out. That was the case with my friend, he didn't have hope and he couldn't see a way out of a life of crime so he lashed out at me for wanting to change my life. It wasn't until much later when he was ready for that shift that he reached out to me and acknowledged that I made the right choice to pursue a better life. You have bigger things to do in this world and it will require you to walk your own path. Some of the people closest to you will not understand why you are making the choices you are making to move your life forward, nor should they, it is YOUR life. They may or may not get on board and encourage and support you in the future, but if they don't you still have to take action and keep going. Your journey to living a purpose-filled life, an exciting life, a life of happiness is what you should be focused on if that is what you want.

My virtual mentor Les Brown is one of the top motivational speakers in the world. He is the author of several New York Times Best Selling books and at one time he was one of the highest paid speakers in the world. I have been following his work for years and one of the things he says often is; you have greatness within you, you have something special. I agree. Never settle for being a passenger in your life, be the driver of your destiny. Know that you have gifts, talents and a greater purpose to do more, give more, share more and your life will change forever.

If I can go from a housing project, headed down the wrong path, to author and speaker overcoming various obstacles, anything is possible for you! You are the driver of your life. You have the ability to do things you never thought possible. You have talents and gifts that need to be shared with the world. Go out in the world, find your gift and share it with the world.

PRINCIPLES FROM DANNY'S STORY:

PRINCIPLE 1:

Never Be Afraid To Walk Your Own Path In Life

You are often faced with challenges and often those challenges take you away from your values and beliefs and who you are meant to be. You go to a job every day that may or may not bring you satisfaction. You may struggle in your relationships, have financial problems or have some things happen to you that are difficult to get over. You may find it difficult to get back on track and everyone around you may be telling you what you should do or how you should live. Maybe you have goals and dreams and you are afraid to chase your greatness. Never be afraid.

PRINCIPLE 2:

You Are Who You Spend Time With The Most

Who are you spending most of your time with? Are they positive, goal-getters? Are they people that are chasing their goals and dreams and encourage you to do the same? Or are they pessimists, who often see the negative side in most things? Do they discourage you from going after what you want and tell you all of the reasons it won't work? Are they leading you down a path that you know is not meant for you?

These are questions you need to ask yourself. If you are not motivated to follow your dreams or to become the best version of yourself, look around you and see who you are spending time with. The people you spend most of your time with influence who you are and what you do. If you are seeking more out of life then it's important to spend time with people who are doing the same. If you don't have people in your life who encourage you, lift you up and hold you accountable for taking action on what you want, seek them out. Find mentors and coaches in your community or online. Go to networking events, find people who are on a similar journey in life and connect with them. Your life will shift in a very powerful and positive way.

PRINCIPLE 3:

Be Careful Who You Confide In About Your Goals & Dreams

This is aligned with who you associate with most; however, it needs to be broken down even more because it is a little different. Many people get excited about a goal that they want to achieve, it could be a recent goal or something they have always wanted. They are ready to take action and begin to take steps to make it happen and they tell their family members, friends, co-workers, children, spouse, boyfriend or girlfriend about their goal. Then what happens is they don't get the response they expect. Instead, they get a negative response, one that discourages them from taking action or moving forward so they quit. Be careful who you tell your goals and dreams to. Only tell your goals to people who you know will support you, encourage you and hold you accountable for taking action. It may be difficult for you not to discuss your goals with those close to you, however, if they have not been supportive in the past or you know they are likely to not support you now, don't tell them. You can show them with your actions, but you must seek out mentors, coaches or people close to you that you know want to see you win.

DANNY STONE

Danny is an author, speaker, success coach, teacher, and community servant that has dedicated his life to helping people see possibilities and take massive action to change their lives. His book, "You Have the Keys, Now Drive" has garnered readers from seven countries thus far. As a seasoned facilitator and speaker, he has delivered hundreds of engaging keynote speeches and seminars on various personal development topics from finding your true purpose, to defining your success, to being the driver of your life. Danny's mission is to teach people how to create more freedom and abundance in their lives.

Website: iamDannyStone.com

Social Media: @iamDannyStone

CHAPTER TWO

SEARCHING FOR IDENTITY & ACCEPTANCE

BY JERMAINE SPENCE

It was the winter of 1988 when I arrived in Canada with my father, I remember the plane landing and feeling a sense of relief that I was finally not in Jamaica anymore. I was finally away from the trouble, away from the pain and hurt; I was finally going to start a new life in a new country with my father. Prior to my arrival in Canada, I waited five years for my father's return to Jamaica. As the years passed, I thought he might never come back for me. My father worked in the trade field as a tool and die worker and I was told that he went to Canada to make a better life for me. My father finally returned to Jamaica when I was eight years old and I remember feeling a great sense of relief that I was no longer going to be living on the streets with my mother. I was so happy to be away from Jamaica, I had no idea this was going to be the last time I would see my mother. I mean, I was glad that I didn't have to struggle anymore because when I lived in Jamaica I remember my mother and I being homeless. My mother lost her home and we had to sleep on couches and depended on the kindness of others to survive. I was so happy and relieved that I no longer had to face those struggles anymore, it was all over now. When I arrived in Canada at the age of eight, I grew up in a tough part of the city called Jane and Finch on a street named Driftwood Avenue.

I was glad Jamaica was behind me and I was looking forward to start a new life in a new country. While living in Driftwood I found myself trying to fit in, trying to be a part of the community but I quickly realized that being a part of the community was not always a positive thing. I quickly found myself involved with people who would lead me down a path of negative attitudes and behaviors. That negative attitude and behavior had me labelled by the school as a problem child. I was placed in a special classroom for kids with behavioral problems and learning disabilities; I was labelled hyperactive and felt I had no choice but to fit the description handed to me. It was not easy growing up in Jane and Finch especially when I was in the community. I saw a lot of violence and witnessed robberies, fights and friends arrested at a young age. Things were not easy for my family, and me so my dad moved us out of Driftwood to Christie and Bloor which is downtown Toronto. While living in the Christie and Bloor area things did not get any better. You see, I was getting older and my attitude got worse. My bad attitude didn't help with my relationship with my stepmom, I wanted to get along with her but there always seemed to be something preventing the connection from happening. My dad married my stepmom before I arrived in Canada and at first, our relationship was really good. I mean, I was happy that I had her as a mother figure; then suddenly her attitude towards me began to change and she started to treat me as if I was an outsider. While growing up she made it very clear I was not going to be anything in life. She used to lock me out of the house whenever I came home late and would always tell me I was not allowed to go into the fridge or eat unless she prepared the meals. This was hard for a growing teenage boy who was always hungry. I really wished she cared about me but it was quite evident by her actions that I was not her priority. At this point feeling rejected became a harsh reality, I've always wanted to be accepted and I've always wanted to be loved but unfortunately I was not going to get it from her. I don't know why, but she just didn't like me and I never got along with her. I could talk about the abuse and the negative words that were spoken to me, for example: I was told that I was never going to be anything in life and that I was going to be dead by the time I was 25. Those are hard words to hear for a 16 year old and I started to believe them. I believed I was going to be "a nobody" and I started to believe that I was going to be nothing but a thug, problem child with no future. I accepted those words and because of my acceptance, it led me down the path of anger and feelings of rejection. I was 16 years old turning 17, was not happy with my life, felt alone and never told anyone that I was always thinking about my mother I left behind. I used to daydream about her wishing she were here with me. As the years went by, I began to wonder if she was dead or alive. I mean I've been in Canada now over 10 years and I've not heard from her since I came off the plane. No contact information, no letters, no phone calls. Not knowing what was going on drove me crazy. As time went by I started to forget about the idea of having a mother or even a family because nobody cared about me, so why should I care about them.

Things started to go downhill when my stepmom and I finally got to a place of no return. I was 16 now and tired of the verbal and physical abuse. It was the summer of 1995, I remember coming home late in the evening and sitting down to eat dinner; while I was eating my stepmother took my plate of food and threw it in the garbage. I don't know if it was because I was tired of being pushed around or had enough of all the insults, put downs and verbal abuse. In seconds, I started to raise my voice then she began to yell and before I knew it, she began to hit me uncontrollably. I really didn't want to hit her back because I knew if I did I would hurt her so I focused my anger towards stuff in the house. I remember kicking the freezer then going into my room, ripping the door off the panel and slamming what was left of my bedroom door in her face as she trailed behind me. I remember feeling tired, hopeless and angry. I wished I could talk to someone but I had no one, not even my dad. He was always at work and when he was around, he acted as if he didn't care. I went to bed that night not realizing what the morning was going to bring. I woke up to a knock at my bedroom door and it was the police telling me that I needed to leave. I looked at them puzzled and said, "I'm 16 years old and I live here." The police told me that my stepmom called and she was afraid for her life and I needed to leave the home. Confused and hurt, I left with nothing but the shorts and t-shirt I was wearing. Kicked out of my house onto the streets with nowhere to go. But that wasn't it, the whole time the police were removing me from my home, my dad was in the other room and it hurt that he knew I was leaving and did not say anything. He didn't come talk to me, he didn't stop the police, he said nothing. He just stayed in the room as I was leaving.

Now I was on the streets homeless for the second time in my life. Feeling as if this was going to be my future. Sleeping on park benches alone and feeling rejected with nowhere to go and no family, feeling as if no one loved me or cared. I also stopped caring. I walked around with an "I have nothing to lose" attitude and that was when I started my journey of searching for acceptance and belonging. Unfortunately, along the way the people who I received acceptance from were not the type of people you would want to be involved with. They showed me love and acceptance. The street accepted me more than my family. I began selling marijuana and crack laced marijuana because I needed to eat. Where was I going to find a job? I had no home address. I sold drugs to survive, to gain acceptance and to fit in because that's what we did on the streets. I had no care and no hope in the world; I felt my only option was to resort to drugs and violence. The crew of fellas I found myself hustling with, we called ourselves the Lost Boys / Hoodlums because we were a bunch of guys that felt lost and rejected. Nobody wanted us or cared about us. We created havoc in the city of Toronto. We used to hang around malls and shopping centers robbing and beating people on the subways sometimes for no reason. Random acts of violence was our calling card, our only care was to sell as much drugs as we could. We went to clubs only to fight people, I felt trapped in a whirlwind. I just did not care about life, "Why should I?" Nobody cared about me. Nobody loved me. I was on a path of destruction a path that would eventually lead me to a point of no return. I was lost. I was angry and confused. I truly felt like nobody wanted me or cared about me. That was my mantra, which was what fueled my actions. Now I was all in; I could feel my days slipping away and being steps away from being criminally charged or going to jail. I was next because many of my friends were in jail, dead or charged and I was on that path. I truly felt that was my future.

While I was living the street life, I attended Central Tech High School and played football. I was an okay football player and I thought that maybe I could get a scholarship to get out of the mess I was in. I would often have dreams that maybe somebody would see me play as a superstar and rescue me from all this violence and madness but it never happened, nobody came to save me. Things began to change when one day my friends and I were walking in the alley by the school when in the distance we saw a few guys from a rival gang standing in front of us. They had mean looking, loud barking pit bulls, but there were only three of them and there were 10 of us. I thought this was going to be an easy fight, I didn't know it would be a defining moment that would change my life forever. As we began to walk towards them, we took out our machetes and knives. We were ready to fight. Little did we know it was a trap; there was at least 20 guys behind us, they surrounded us and they also had weapons. I didn't know what to do, the only thing that was going through my head was I'm either going to get out or I'm going to die. The brawl began and as we were fighting, I watched many of my friends get stabbed repeatedly. I was helpless because I was also being attacked. I didn't know what to do. All I saw was my life flashing before my eyes. In the moment it all came rushing back like an old rerun; I saw the days of being homeless with my mother in Jamaica, I saw my stepmom cursing me and the words, "I was never going to be anything." At that point, my only thought was I have to get out of this situation alive. It all happened so quickly and I had no idea how bad it was, I looked around and we were all bleeding and hurt. A few people were on the ground, I didn't know if my friends were dead or alive. Someone called 911, while some friends lay on the ground motionless; others limped away before the police could arrive. The alley turned crime scene was covered in blood. I had mixed emotions that night as I was nursing my wounds, luckily enough, I only suffered a few scars on my back and 8 stitches over my eye; unfortunately some of the guys in my crew were not as lucky. I didn't know if I wanted to end my life or get revenge. I didn't know what to do. With revenge in my heart, I turned to the biggest thug on the streets. He was one of the hardest street thugs I rolled with so I knew he would have what I desired at that moment. I went to his house and asked him to give me a gun. I was confused, angry and I was going to get revenge. What happened next totally changed my path and my mind forever. My friend looked at me and rather than give me "the piece" that he often travelled with or "the backups", he stashed away in his apartment; he looked me in the eyes and said, "Jermaine I'm not going to give you the gun, this is not you." I was so confused! I mean he was a thug just like me; what do you mean this is not me. This is me! "I'm a nobody, a street kid, nobody loves me, I'm good for nothing, I'm going to be dead by the time I'm 25, it's me! Please give me the gun!!" He said, "No." I walked away that night troubled and filled with turmoil. I thought, "What's next. I can't do this anymore, I can't be like this anymore. My life has to change."

That night I sat alone in my room contemplating my life. Wondering if I should continue to live this messed up life of violence, rejection with no hope. I had no idea what to do and my only conclusion was to take my life. However, in the back of my mind I felt like, if I was to die no one would care. I felt it would not matter. People may cry for the moment, but for the most part they would move on with their lives. In that dark place, I felt something inside telling me if I killed myself I would be killing my future.

It was at that point I knew there was more, even though society and my family looked at me in a negative way, I knew that there was good in me and I could make a difference in this world. I just needed to believe it.

I was physically 19 but on the inside, I realized I was a little boy hurting and lost in a world that didn't accept me. I recognized that I had to cut off the people around me, the crew that had my back in the streets. They did not have my best interest at heart. I was ready to change the people I was around and the things I used to do. My journey began and I spent the next few years trying to find myself. I had enough of the violence, the drugs and being lost with no direction. Now I was ready to accept that I needed to live differently and the way I was living in the past was only going to lead me down a path of destruction. My spiritual journey began when I was truly empty and alone. For some strange reason call it destiny or purpose I kept meeting people who were Christians. They would always invite me to church and at first, I was skeptical because I wanted nothing to do with religion.

Even though I was empty and lost, I knew there was more to my life. One thing that intrigued me about church was the community within the environment; a family, something that I longed for since childhood. I was alone and felt like nobody wanted me. My birth mom disappeared on me, my dad disowned me and my stepmom hated me and wanted nothing to do with me. Only the church showed me love, gave me a family and a sense of community. As I grew in my relationship with God things started to get real and church became more than a religious institution to me. It became a way of living. I developed a relationship with God that totally transformed my life. My favourite line when growing up was, "I'll figure it out." My whole life I've tried to make things happen in my own strength and power but always came up short. Until one day, God showed me that I couldn't do it on my own and I needed God's strength and wisdom to help me manage my life. I also realized that coming from a place of rejection led to the feeling that no one cared about me, not even God. As I began to build a relationship with God, he revealed to me his presence and the power to recover from the pain and rejection from my past. I had to commit all my life and will to Christ's care and control. Then allow God to examine me and ask to reveal the things that will help me to confess my faults. God changed my heart and brought me to a place where I was humble enough to work on my character defects.

Throughout my newly found relationship with God, I learned that the principle of forgiveness is what leads to healing. Someone once told me that "un-forgiveness" and hatred is like drinking poison and wishing the other person death. I was drinking the poison and it was killing me, I had to let the people that have hurt me go. I had to forgive them. The forgiveness was more for me to release my hatred than to let them off the hook. The pent-up anger was hurting me a lot more than it was hurting them. I came to the point where I realized it's not about what they did to me, it's about my reaction to what they did and what I allowed to affect me. I had to let it go. I learned that people that hurt you are often those same people who have been hurt themselves. I finally understood that forgiveness is an attitude and a perspective. I began to spend time with God daily for self-examination. As I spent time with God, He began to give me the power to understand why the people who hurt me did what they did. I was looking for love, I wanted my stepmom to love me, I wanted my dad to be there when I needed him, I wanted my real mom to be in my life. However, I came to the realization that the things I wanted from these individuals was not realistic, because they just did not have it to give me. I started to understand that you could not get something from someone if they don't have it; they cannot give you what they don't have. One of the things I had to realize at a young age is that I can't fix other people. I can only work on myself and control how I react to what other people have done to me.

When I think about my journey, I can see myself as the little boy searching and wondering where he was going to find what he needed out of life but all the while the answer was within him. I've been through a lot of close calls, I've almost made decisions that would have drastically changed the direction of my life, but through it all I know God's hands were on me. I know God was with me in the good and the bad times. When I thought I was going to die and I had no food to eat, God was with me. I will never forget when I asked my friend for the gun. I mean, why didn't he give it to me? What stopped him? There was no reason for him to look at me and say, "No." There was no reason for him to say, "Jermaine that is not you." I remember reading in the bible about God protecting those he loves and I remember someone saying to me, that when we're not thinking about God he's thinking about us. To me that was a prime example of God thinking about someone who at the time did not care to know a God he did not believe in. Now when I think about that situation I realize that God had his hands on my life. If my friend had given me the gun that night, I would never have the life that I have today. I would never have met the love of my life that I've been married to for the last 14 years. I would have never had three healthy and beautiful children. I would never have become the advocate for homeless men and for those who suffer from mental health illness and of course, I wouldn't be a contributor to this book.

The principle of forgiveness has allowed me to soften my heart to the people who at one time I believed hurt me the most. After 32 years of not seeing or hearing from my mother, I actually had the opportunity to sit down and talk with her on a recent trip to Jamaica. My wife met her mother-in-law and my kids met grandma for the first time. I had a million questions but at the end of the interaction I concluded that she did what she thought was best at the time. Our relationship is a work in progress but would have never started if it wasn't for the principle of forgiveness.

My father and I have found a way to resolve some of our issues. Although we aren't as close as I would like I have found a way to release the anger I had for him and to love him in the place where he is. Again not a perfect relationship, not even close, but it's better than it was the day I was escorted out of his house. My stepmom and I probably had the most opposing relationship of them all. Funny enough, throughout my childhood I would often feel disapproval and resentment from her. I would wonder if my father ever sensed her tension towards me but his silence had me feeling that maybe it was just in my head. Funny enough, 25 years after kicking me out of her house, in a rare moment of openness my stepmom turned to me one day and said, "I'm sorry." I heard her voice and saw her mouth move, but those words coming from her were as rare as a solar eclipse. I asked her to repeat herself and again she said, "I'm sorry." As simple as she could, for the first time, my stepmother admitted that during my childhood she wasn't always as nice to me as she could have been. She knew she was wrong and felt it in her heart to apologize. At that moment, I recognized that she too had found the principle of forgiveness.

By no means am I perfect. I still got a lot to work on. The one thing I know is I can only live life one day at a time, one minute at a time, one second at a time. What I do in those minutes, in those seconds will eventually affect my day which will eventually affect my week which will eventually affect my month which will eventually affect my future. I'm still searching, but now I have tools with me this time around and I have faith that God will never leave me nor forsake me and will always be there for me as I move forward towards this next chapter in my life.

I've been through a lot and I know that what I've been through made me who I am. However, I understand that I cannot use where I've been to take me where I need to go.

PRINCIPLES FROM JERMAINE'S STORY:

PRINCIPLE 1:

You Cannot Control How Others May Treat You

You cannot control how others may treat you; however, you can only control your response to their treatment. The one thing life has taught me is that when it rains everyone gets wet; we can't control the weather; however you can control your reaction to the bad weather.

PRINCIPLE 2:

"Un-Forgiveness" Is Like Drinking Poison While Wishing The Other Person Death

The more I drank the poison of "un-forgiveness" the more it was killing me on the inside. "Un-forgiveness" did nothing for me but cause me to consume my pains and damage my life, which hurt people around me.

PRINCIPLE 3:

The Road You Choose

When I was at the darkest point in my life, I began to contemplate my purpose and my place in this world; during my time of contemplation, two thoughts came to mind.

1) If I killed myself people would cry for the

moment but would eventually move on with their lives and I would be nothing more than a memory. 2) Killing myself would mean I would be killing my future. The pain I was feeling would still be with me in death.

PRINCIPLE 4:

I Developed A Relationship With God That Totally Transformed My Life

My relationship with God brought me to a place of admitting I was powerless to control my tendencies to do the wrong things and without God my life was unmanageable. The bible says in **Proverbs 3:5-6 (NKJV) Verse 5:** *Trust in the Lord with all your heart, And lean not on your own understanding; Verse 6: In all your ways acknowledge Him, And He shall direct your paths.*

PRINCIPLE 5:

Love Them For They Are

The Lord Showed Me That My Dad and Stepmother Couldn't Give Me What They Did Not Have. My frustration with my parents was that I wanted something from them that they could not give. The Lord showed me to love and accept them for who they were.

JERMAINE SPENCE

Jermaine Spence works as a Community Support Worker for the Canadian Mental Health Association in Peel, which is within the Greater Toronto area. Jermaine is also the founder and operator of a social initiative called "Hope Endoors Community Services", which provides transitional housing support for men suffering from mental health and addictions issues. Jemaine is an ordained pastor and serves as the Young Adult Pastor of Dayspring Church in Brampton Ontario.

CHAPTER THREE

THIS GAME CALLED LIFE, WHICH YOU CAN'T PLAY TWICE

BY JAMAL CAMPBELL

My name is Jamal Campbell. This is my story. I am a professional football player for the Toronto Argonauts of the Canadian Football League (CFL). I am a recent York University Alum, graduating with Honours in Sociology. Getting to where I am today was not easy. It took a lot of perseverance, faith, focus, discipline and hard work.

Growing up in inner city Toronto was a blessing but it had its challenges like any urban big city. As a young black male, I had to learn how to trust in my Faith, rely on self-determination and my work ethic to reach success. Being raised in a low-income single-parent household, I was exposed first-hand to some of the circumstances that follow. My mom raised my older sister, two younger brothers and myself — all of different fathers primarily in the Jane and Finch area. The media has labelled this area of Toronto as the notorious hub spot for drugs and street gang activity. Many of the residents of the neighborhood come from an immigrant background. To me, Jane and Finch is a wonderful community. I see it as a community fueled by culture. It's a place in the city where you can order Caribbean, African, Vietnamese, Chinese, Sri Lankan and Latino food all at one intersection. It's a community of hard workers, people that are always hustling always moving and trying to get things done. Artistic expression is visible throughout the neighbourhoods; the murals are decorated with positive messages. There is a legacy of musical artistry from Jane and Finch paving the way for the success and recognition young artists are receiving now in Canada and internationally. Growing up here and having all of the support from the residents who love the community also motivates these artists to stay focused. Kids just want to be kids in any neighborhood in the city; the kids in this neighborhood just have to learn how to move differently. The youth in our neighborhood are faced with challenges that give them the opportunity to grow, which they might not necessarily have to face if their socio-economic status was different. For instance, the image of youth walking under yellow police tape in December of 2018 after being in lockdown at Firgrove elementary school because of a drive-by shooting that occurred on school property. As a child when you are raised in an environment as such, survival is on your mind every day. This limits children from reaching their full potential because they're worried about potential situations no child in Canada should have to worry about. I personally think growing up in this type of environment prepares you for the world.

You might ask how a single mom, working 2 jobs was able to adequately raise four children on her own. I'm old enough now to understand how hard it must have been for my mom. We leaned heavily on family and the welfare system for support. From living in a shelter, to living in Toronto community housing, to living with my grandma when we were evicted. For many years, we had to depend on food banks and other generous charities to provide us with food security. My mom had to play the role of both mother and father and as you could imagine that's quite the task when raising four energetic kids in a community surrounded with opportunities to engage in potential harm. Raised in a single parent household was common amongst my group of friends; mostly single moms. We would joke about being "bastards". Looking back now maybe that was just the way we coped with having that absence.

When we study the family as an institution, we commonly think that the normal family consists of two parents with children (nuclear family). In my community, these households are far from the norm. Typically, we are raised by one parent or by grandparents. The result, family responsibilities are very different to the average nuclear family. Personally, my mom worked two jobs most of the time so my sister and I took care of our younger brothers. The strain that a single parent faces through social, financial and emotional circumstances leaves a residual effect on the children in this type of environment. Day-to-day survival is the mindset of these parents versus long-term growth. Whether it is providing food, clothing, shelter or safety for their children, some of the less emphasized routines are neglected. The mindset of desperation takes over in this environment. Choices are made that seem to be in the best interest for short-term survival. There is little to no focus on the future; this often leaves young kids uninspired and disadvantaged. Instead of saving and investing in their children's future, parents are working long hours living paycheck to paycheck. When a parent with no spousal support is occupied working instead of caring for her/his children, it creates the potential for young kids to be raised by the streets. Young boys longing for the sense of belonging and identity, learning the ways of how to provide from the older heads on the block. Young girls taken advantage of, looking for love in all the wrong places. I witnessed this. This was my reality. The scary thing is that history repeats itself if there is no intervention. We learned these ways of living from what we've seen; our parents learned these ways from what they've seen. If we don't commit to educating our communities and ourselves our children will continue to be influenced by what they've seen.

When I was in elementary school, I could remember my mom not allowing me to play outside with the other boys, because she didn't want us running the streets late night with no purpose. She was afraid of the trouble I might get into. At the time, I didn't understand that she was just trying to protect me from making foolish mistakes, which would hinder me in the future. Some of those same friends got into trouble with the law at a very young age and this only justified her reasoning. I was never the type of kid to follow what the crowd was doing. However we were so young and misguided, all of us trying to find ourselves in a world with no real positive male role models, it was only inevitable that trouble would find us. I often look at myself today and think; how was I so fortunate to have a mother who drained so much of her own energy trying to keep us out the streets? I also wonder about some of my other friends who weren't so fortunate. Where would they be today if they had that support and didn't become a product of the environment? I truly believe that every kid can become anything he/she chooses to become, but that kid has to receive a fair opportunity to realize his/her own potential.

By middle school, I already started to understand the influence that our environment had on us as kids. We had all these misconceptions of what we thought was important at the time. Rappers and figures that made a lot of quick flashy money influenced us. At 12 years old, the only thing I was concerned with was having a pair of Jordan's, and a pair of Dickies (pants) at the time that was the style. This was the way to fit in with the other boys. The most important feeling at that age was feeling like I belonged. I remember being a part of a group of boys in seventh grade and we used to go around fighting and causing trouble, for no particular reason. I didn't really enjoy the fighting, but it was a way for us to feel like we were respected. We always felt like we had to prove ourselves. We used to go by the plaza at lunchtime and that's what we seen the high school kids doing. Being in middle school my mom allowed me more time after school to hang out with friends. At this age, I had already seen some of my friends recruited into gangs, selling drugs, using drugs and carrying weapons. One evening when we were playing basketball on the courts across the street from my building a young man was shot in his face broad day light. I believe he survived. My mom went back to trying to keep us inside our home. I think she thought that she would be able to better protect us that way, but truth is when you are in an environment like this you're going to be exposed to the elements regardless. After that day, my mom once again tried everything she could to control my siblings and our movement. It was very easy to go against our mother's wishes because she was always working late into the evening and by the time she got home, she was focused on making dinner and trying to relax from a hard day's work. At this point in my life the violence in Jane and Finch was at a high and it didn't seem like it would get any better. These were the days of the hood famous rappers putting on for their blocks and the messages they were rapping about obviously played out in the streets. Regardless of all of this, I still limited my involvement in all of this chaos, probably because I knew my mom would discipline me if I ever were caught. My mom saw the value in education. She would always be engaged in our parent-teacher interviews, but she didn't have the time to make sure that we were doing our homework because of her schedule, still she tried.

High school was an interesting time in my adolescence. I've learned some of life's most valuable lessons by witnessing my peers interact on a daily basis. I attended C. W. Jeffery's (CWJ) in 2008 the year after the unfortunate incident where a 15-year old named Jordan Manners had his life taken due to gun violence. This was a countrywide story covered by most major media outlets. This was alarming to the country and city residents, because he was the first victim to die of this kind of violence on school grounds in Toronto. My mom was hesitant to let me attend school there. Councilors and the administration did an adequate job of insuring student safety after this incident. The truth is this could've happened at any of the schools in priority neighborhoods at the time. This stage in my life is where I learned who I wanted to be. In ninth grade, I was socially diverse. I was hanging out with friends that I knew from middle school, students I just met that year and prospective athletes. I was never an A+ student, so I wasn't drawn to the academic kids but I was cool with them. I realized that it only got harder trying to avoid unfavorable situations that might get me into trouble. In high school, we had more freedom and more choices. Without that structure of guidance, we would have to learn from our own mistakes or the ones we seen from others. As a young male in this environment, you almost become desensitized to seeing gang violence, weapons and drugs on a daily basis. I had no need to be a part of this, so it was never really a hard choice for me to just be a witness and not partake.

By the tenth grade, I had seen enough to realize that I wanted to make the best out of my life. I saw people shot, stabbed, robbed, beat viscously and drugged out. I wanted no part of it. Everyday I'd see boys my age with the designer clothes, the bands of cash, the freshest shoes and the ladies. I looked up to them because they had the respect. On the flipside, their lives were always threatened. That's what made me not want to be like them. In this environment, one thing was consistent: we didn't have many solid positive male role models around us to show us that there was more to life. For the men that tried to be these role models, it was easy to rebel against them. As a fatherless young man you walk around with this attitude, "I don't have no dad, so I'm not going to let no man talk to me like he's my dad." It's an ignorant way of thinking, but at that age we thought it was the right mindset.

We were told that a man makes his own decisions, which is true; but a real man makes the best decisions for himself and for his family.

That's where we had it confused. It was easy for us to act out the stigmas portrayed about us; we behaved the way everyone expected us to behave. It was almost easier that way. When people don't expect much from you, you tend to not expect much from yourself and because of this we were able to get a lot of handouts and take advantage of people's kindness.

For us young boys growing up in Jane and Finch, we were never exposed to thinkers that would elevate our minds for the long term. People who wanted to help us were mostly there temporarily. Sometimes it was community outreach organizations or afterschool programs. We used to go to these programs after school for the free pizza and the free bus tickets. These people that were trying to help us cared more about our future than we did. We were disrespectful, not appreciative of these resources because we didn't care. The only success that we ever envisioned was playing sports or doing music.

It was sports that changed my life forever! Before I got involved with sports, I was just a misguided, unmotivated, insecure and rebellious teen trying to live day by day with no goals. I thought that when I was done with high school I was going to be a construction worker at best. After witnessing all of these negative experiences and now starting to envision a future different from what I seen, I committed myself. I've always been a competitor; I think that comes from living in an environment where we always have to prove ourselves. We would compete against each other and not collaborate with each other. Growing up, if a boy seen you with a nice watch, instead of coming up to you and saying, "Brother that's a nice watch, how did you get it? How could I get one myself? Could you show me how to get one?" it was easier for that boy to see your nice watch and instead of admiring it, he would try to take it from you. As a community, we were divided and we didn't know how to work together; even on team sports we were selfish. Everyone wanted to take the shots, but no one wanted to pass the ball, even if it meant losing the game. If you allow it to, this mindset translates to all aspects of one's life.

I got involved with basketball and wrestling. When I started out I wasn't very athletic and I wasn't very good but it filled a void inside of me that I didn't know existed. Back then, I remember being the slowest runner, but I also remember pushing myself so hard. So hard that in 2016 I tested first overall in the CFL 40-yard dash at my position. An opponent tried to demean me and curse at me, but I never responded, I just told myself that I was going to be the best one day. At basketball? At wrestling? I didn't know and to be honest, it didn't matter. For the first time in my life, I had a reason to believe in myself and I truly loved that feeling. As I got better, I was happier I always wanted to improve. I used to wake up at 6am for basketball practices in the morning, more basketball at lunch, basketball afterschool and travelled to practice two times a week to a neighborhood named Parkdale. An area that was just as familiar as my neighborhood. It was quite a travel just to bounce a ball, but the truth is that was the spot for competitive basketball at that time. I took any opportunity to compete and get better. I even told myself I was going to the NBA. I never did share this with anyone; I just really believed it myself. I didn't know how I was going to get there, but I knew that if I continued to work harder than everyone and get better at every chance, I would make it. For this found passion, I thank my basketball coach "BEAST". A nickname he picked up for dominating ball courts in his time, but carried over to his coaching style. Through coach's tough love approach, I learned a number of valuable lessons that continue to stay with me today. Some of which were, how to not victimize myself (because the world didn't feel sorry for me), never get complacent and dedicate myself to what I want. By the time I was 16 years old, I was so confident, that I believed that anything I put my hands on would lead to success. Some might call it a false sense of confidence, but this allowed me to get to where I am today.

Although my love for basketball remained strong, little did I know that another sport would come along and truly steal my heart. The first time I encountered football was through the CFL's Toronto Argonauts "level the playing field" initiative, a program intended to grow the sport within the inner city. For kids like us, we couldn't afford to play football. We only really ever played basketball and soccer so this was an opportunity of a lifetime that I wasn't planning to miss. I remember the Argos invited us to attend one of their home games and we got to run out of the tunnel alongside the players as they stormed onto the field. That feeling was amazing and as young as I was, I knew I wanted to experience that as a professional player one day. Running on that field as a child, being escorted by gladiators in football uniforms was exciting, but watching these giants play was a feeling all onto itself. Something that for the very first time I pictured myself doing. The first time I put football pads on, I remember looking at myself in the mirror and imagined playing in the pros. In my head, I was the best player there was. Funny enough when I look back now I can admit that I wasn't very good, but one thing for sure I always gave it my all. I had the motor and no matter how many times it felt like I was running into a wall (opposing players) I would try to run through that wall again and again and again. I carried this mindset with me from high school all the way to when I attended York University. I remember weighing in at 215 pounds; my first year was rough at this weight playing defensive end, for university football standards. I was redshirted (sat out the year to develop my body and skill); that discouraged some players. It actually motivated me. I worked so hard my first off-season; I put on 65lbs in that one year and became a starter the following season. That entire off-season I worked extremely hard. Every day I repeated my saying that I came up with in high school when I was training intensely to reach my fitness goals. I told myself every day to push myself more, "My Motivation is My Determination." Putting in all that work and dedicating myself as a student athlete taught me so many invaluable lessons. Some of these lessons that I still use today are, "You can have whatever you want in this life, if you're willing to work for it" and, "Hard work always pays off." I focused so much on my craft, that some might have said I was selfish. Well, I understand how important the moment is and knowing this I will not let the moment pass. The moment to me represents an opportunity. Sometimes you only get one opportunity in life, while others in your same situation don't even receive an opportunity. Every day we're blessed with opportunities, how we choose to use them is our individual choice. My trust in God allows me to stay focused on my goals. I wasn't concerned about things, small things, things that really didn't matter. All that mattered to me was my dreams and I focused on nothing else but accomplishing my dreams. I knew that I had to take control of the controllable and if I did that, everything else would work out.

On May 10th 2016, everything that I worked so hard for was finally manifesting. It was CFL Draft day and I was at home with family and friends, not knowing what was going to happen. I performed well at the CFL National Combine weeks before, testing first place in four out of six events used to judge athletic performance in potential draft picks. My agent and I spoke with a few teams that were interested, who saw me as a raw player with a lot of potential. I remember the first two rounds went by and my name wasn't called. I was anxious and nervous, at the same time trying to remain calm, bracing for whatever was going to happen. I still kept my faith, prayed and patiently waited. Then the moment came, "with the 22nd selection in the 2016 CFL draft," the announcer said, "the Toronto Argonauts select offensive lineman Jamal Campbell." The house erupted in cheers and for the first three minutes, they all hugged me so hard that I missed the first phone call from the Argos organization congratulating me on their selection. Not only was I selected in the draft, but also by the team, that first introduced me to football. I thanked God. I was filled with so much emotion, gratitude and also a sense of responsibility. I was now a professional football player, playing within my own city, a city that raised me. A city where I could continue to make a powerful impact as a role model to kids and young people who grew up like myself. To be the type of player I looked up to when I was a kid, someone who could make a great impact on the field and a long-lasting influence within the community. Off the field, I knew that there was going to be hard work ahead and I was willing to go as hard as necessary. Because of the love and dedication to sport that I learned so long ago, it had prepared me to make the job in the pros.

"My Motivation is my Determination" was not just a catchy rhyming phrase that I made up in high school; it's a personal motto that was developed from the depths of my being. A phrase that I used when I was most challenged both physically and mentally, when things got extremely hard. When some of my friends were chilling and I had to go to practice, or when my body wanted to quit, but I had to work out, in every one of those exasperated moments, I knew that my motivation had to come from my determination. My determination to make something out of myself. In the coldest and loneliest of times, to the happiest and easiest of times, I tell myself this same phrase every single day. What motivated me was my determination for wanting to be the best that I can be. This was particularly true with the first time I ran a four km run, and I felt like passing out. I repeated my motto to myself over and over and over and over. Anytime I faced adversity, I spoke these words to myself, "My Motivation is my Determination." I knew I couldn't quit! My mom never quit. She didn't quit on life and she sure didn't quit on me. After many years I realized, it wasn't about me, it was about doing this thing called life for my mom. I remember when I was about five years old, my sister and I would sit in on my mom's college classes, because she had no one else to watch us. Some of her fellow classmates would look at us weird, because they didn't understand that she couldn't afford childcare. She didn't have to finish her schooling, but she did! She didn't quit! So how could I quit! She was able to receive her diploma in social services, while parenting us all on her own. I watched my mom be the victim of domestic violence, both emotional and physical from multiple men in our lives, she still didn't quit! I watched my mom provide for us when we were homeless and there was no hope, she still didn't quit! So who am I to quit, when all I had to do was believe and know that MY MOTIVATION IS MY DETERMINATION!

The craziest thing to me is that I grew up with so many talented young men and women around me. The individuals that had the physical ability to compete in any sport, to go on and do greater things, but they didn't have the mindset. They didn't have the guidance, the focus and the determination to want the best for themselves. I was fortunate enough to have teachers believe in me, coaches who challenged my ignorant ways of thinking, pushing me to envision a life beyond the stereotypes. They made me see a life more impactful than sports and to understand the importance of education. By the time I left high school I understood that my education was something no one could take from me. I thought of these teachers as I thought of my mother. I cared about them, because they cared about me. They made me feel loved and significant. I used to try to just get by in school, but after feeling the love from these teachers; I wanted to strive for the best. Teachers that made such an impact on my life that I wanted to succeed for them, so that I could confirm what they believed about me. These teachers were mother and father figures to me, in high school that type of support was essential to my self-growth. Without these teachers, I wouldn't have been able to see the importance of education. I wouldn't have shifted my mindset in the eleventh grade to strive to attend university. Without university, there would have been no football. I'm grateful beyond words that these gifts of humanity were placed in my life to groom me into the young man who I am today. Why was I so blessed that they were able to influence me? Why me? I don't think it was a coincidence, but you know what, once I knew better, I started to do better. It's a blessing that God gave me physical abilities, but the experiences to foresee a life of accomplishment and success is a greater blessing. One thing will always remain the same, my faith in my Lord and Savior, Jesus Christ.

A once lost young man, who really could have gone the way of destruction, now blessed to make a difference in the lives of others. I once ran on a football field beside gladiators dressed in football uniforms, looking up to them and thinking how amazing they seemed. I am now one of the gladiators. Every time I run out of the locker room in my home city and I see the CN Tower and see the excitedly wide-eyed kids cheer us on as we enter the field, I think to myself, what is this child going through in their life? How will this situation change them? Will they be the next generation to play on this field? I can never really answer those questions, but what I do know is that in every circumstance I have to be that positive influence and role model. I take on that challenge! As I mentioned before, with no intervention in the lives of our young people, history will repeat itself. Blessed to be in a position of influence, I am determined to be that intervention. When not playing football, I often spend time visiting, speaking and mentoring teens and young adults throughout Toronto. I realize that I could have easily gone down a negative path, but because of the love that poured into me I am in my position today. I plan to be that difference to a young man or young woman.

My personal battles included growing up and navigating my way through a tough neighborhood, finding my way to success. Your struggles will be personal to you as well. Your health, your finances, your education, your mental health and so on. Whatever your encounters may be in your life, always know that "Your

Motivation is Your Determination." You have the ability to find your own level of success. The road will not be easy for you. Along your path, you will have distractions, temptations, days that it feels easier to walk away and times you feel like you are too tired to keep going. Know that you cannot quit. Find your reason to keep going and you too will reach your goals. Because I didn't stop, I am not only a professional football player, but I am also a 2017 Grey Cup Champion and as of 2018, I am also a university graduate. Let your determination, the thing that drives you the most be your motivation. I guarantee you will find your own level of success.

PRINCIPLES FROM JAMAL'S STORY

PRINCIPLE 1:

Let Your Motivation Be Your Determination

Wake up every day and attack the day. Focus on the moment. Prepare for the future but enjoy the moment, because the moment is the only thing that is present. Today is the day to become who you want to become. You don't need to depend on the support of others. Do it for yourself! BELIEVE IN YOURSELF! It won't be easy, but look life in the face and embrace adversity!

PRINCIPLE 2:

Control The Controllable

In life there will continue to be many situations you find yourself in that are going to challenge you and even make you question yourself and your ability. It is very important that you give energy to what is worth it. Focus on the areas of your life in which YOU can improve, however little or big it may seem, working daily to improve yourself will bring much joy and success to your life. Go to sleep and rest assured knowing that you did everything that you could do to be a better person today.

PRINCIPLE 3:

Keep Your Faith Strong

Hebrews 13:8 King James Version (KJV) 8 Jesus Christ the same yesterday, and today, and forever. Life is constant, life is moving and life is always changing. People let you down, you let yourself down and you probably let your loved ones down before. One thing that will always be consistent and dependable is the Lord. Whatever your belief is, find time daily to connect with your spirituality and take time throughout the day to give thanks for all of your blessings.

JAMAL CAMPBELL

Since selected in the 2016 CFL draft to play for his home city Toronto Argonauts Football Club, Jamal Campbell is not only a recent graduate of York University earning his BA with honours in Sociology, Jamal is also a 2017 Grey Cup Champion, who uses his blessings to reach the Youth of Toronto.

Jamal is the recipient of the 2017 Toronto Urban Hero Award for his contributions to youth in sport. In 2019, he received the Rotary Club Youth Impact Award. Jamal believes that every child deserves the opportunity to succeed in life. He mentors youth on the importance of education, working hard and staying focused on one's goals to reach one's success.

Social Media: @hestootall

CHAPTER FOUR

THE UGLY GIFT

BY JEFF A. D. MARTIN

Have you ever heard of the term the "Ugly Gift"? It sounds like a bit of a contradiction doesn't it? An oxymoronic phrase? Two words that seem like they should never go together. Ugly, meaning unattractive or unpleasant and a gift, which is something I think we all typically love to receive with open arms. Mash these two opposing words into one expression and you get the receiving of something unpleasant with open arms. Ugh! Even breaking down the term Ugly Gift doesn't make it sound any sweeter, but I do guarantee you this. Even if the term Ugly Gift doesn't have a beautiful ring to it and even if you have never heard of this term prior to today, I will guarantee you that sometime within your life have experienced and have lived through your own personal Ugly Gift. Some of you might just be living in your Ugly Gift right now. I pray that my story brings you some level of understanding to the importance of your own Ugly Gift and how you can use it to live a more purposeful life.

I had a meaningful conversation with someone a few years ago, a discussion I will not soon forget. The topic was about gratitude. We spoke deeply about how life can sometimes bring circumstances that we don't ask for; situations that are difficult, conditions that are tragic and events that are so earth shattering that sometimes you don't even want to get out of bed. Even though we can come face to face with life's adversities, I pointed out that rather than taking the route of tossing our hands in the air to give up the fight, we really should make all attempts to learn within the moment and see what lessons we're able to take away from that circumstance.

"Yes," my friend stated in agreement, "you mean the ugly gift!"

"The ugly gift?" I parroted back, questioning a term I had never heard of prior to the conversation.

"Yes, the ugly gift," he reassured.

"If we view the events that we face every day as gifts, whether they are circumstances we have asked for or not, or if we find pleasure in them or not, each of them are gifts nonetheless."

He went on to explain that some of the gifts we receive are extremely pleasurable and bring us great joy; passing an exam, falling in love, being proposed to, landing that dream job, receiving a promotion, coming into money, finding out you're expecting a baby after multiple failed attempts, receiving a clear bill of health after a cancer scare. All great gifts and all events that many of us would love to receive throughout our lifetime. The ugly gifts however are the events that are less desirable and depending on the depth of its complexities, we really wouldn't wish them on our worst enemy. From the more bearable end of the negative spectrum such as, failing a course in school, losing your cell phone, not getting that raise you hoped for, stubbing your toe, losing your wallet or getting into a minor fender bender. To the utterly terrorizing end of the scale: suffering through a miscarriage, contracting a terminal illness, losing a loved one in a tragic manner, becoming a victim of sexual assault or losing a limb in a freak accident. These ugly gifts that are handed to us, that we are forced to unwillingly receive always arrive at the least opportune time. Not to say that there is ever a good time to accept an ugly gift such as suffering from a brain aneurysm or being held up at gunpoint, but if bad timing isn't enough, these ugly gifts are rarely simple in their solutions. They often come with intricacies and complications that take their recipients out at the knees. These ugly gifts are often delivered to us wrapped in sewage soaked wrapping paper, tied with a fecal matter drenched ribbon, a bow on top that's been injected with snake venom and a delightful gift tag made from arsenic that has your name neatly printed right on it in the most beautiful calligraphic penmanship you've ever seen in your life. Oh... and the ink in the pen used to sign your name is blue coloured rat urine. Yes, this ugly gift is yours for the taking, with no right to refusal. Even though this ugly gift is nothing you would have ever dreamt for yourself, not even in your own worst nightmares, somewhere deep within the repulsive exterior of this gift beyond the excruciating packaging is a silver lining. A lesson, a talent or an endowment that is sitting and waiting for you.

One of the ugliest gifts that I have ever received came to me in 2005. In August of that year, I had one of the happiest moments of my life; however, with the quick swing of a pendulum, I also had one of the most horrific events in my life. After many years of working within pretty much all realms of the security guard field, I made a change. From watching desolate construction sites overnight ensuring no one stole a hammer, to bouncing at nightclubs head locking drunk and belligerent individuals kicking them out before they had the opportunity to swing at me, to prestigious bodyguard work for some of the world's biggest celebrities. I finally made the decision to trade in the pay inconsistency and job instability of security to become a Police Investigator. After many failed attempts, rejection letters, the ignoring of my phone calls, enquiries to the recruiting office after dropping off my sixth resume and even interviewers smirking at my expense through an hour and a half long interview. I was ultimately successful and eventually hired in early 2005. I was ecstatic because I really worked myself up to this career.

Because of the neighbourhood I grew up in, Rexdale a tougher portion of Toronto, any interaction that we young people in the community had with the police was usually negative. I mean, I wasn't blind to the violence, drugs and gangs in my area, but I also saw the beautiful people in an underserved neighbourhood who worked hard and just fought for a better life for themselves and their loved ones. At that time, to me it appeared that the police purposely blinded themselves to the good and only appeared to deal with the bad. However, despite the negative interaction that I would see with the police, at an early age I always noticed the power and influence that they demanded once they stepped into a room. I also recognized how many of them would abuse this power. I always thought to myself, if the police actually used their influence to help bring this community together, how much greater of an impact they could actually have on the youth. Because of this early thinking, and other influences that persuaded me along the way, I decided to make a difference in my community by going the route of becoming an officer.

I had gone through some serious and vigorous training at the police college and had finally completed it. My family and close friends drove down to the college for my graduation. They were so proud to see me in that uniform. After all the sweaty workouts, early morning runs, sleepless study nights and practicing of newly acquired skills I was proud to look at myself in that uniform. Once I graduated from the police college, I went back home early August for more localized training.

On the morning of Monday August 15, 2005, I had planned to go for a morning jog to get my blood circulating and muscles moving before I went into work for more training. I was still so excited because of this new change in my life. A new career meant new opportunities and I was thrilled to meet these new obstacles head on. When my 5:15 AM alarm sounded on my cellphone, which doubled as my alarm clock, I shot up out of bed and grabbed my running gear to get a head start on an already woken and rising sun. Once I was ready to go, I again grabbed for my cellphone that was now tripling as an mp3 player. As I unlocked the phone to start my workout playlist, I noticed missed calls. Calls that came in during the dead of night while I was fast asleep and the phone was set to a silent – do not disturb mode. There were a lot of missed phone calls; 22 to be exact. All came from my younger cousins Kemela and Tanesha whom I am to this day, very close with. I quickly called one of the numbers back and got Kemela. She was crying profusely. It was difficult to hear what she was trying to communicate as her words were muffled by the sounds of her distress. Through her sobbing, she struggled to get the words out, "Omar's been shot, HE'S DEAD!" I heard the words but they didn't make sense. I didn't comprehend what she was trying to tell me about her older brother, my younger cousin. "What?" I asked in disbelief, trying to make sense of her statement. She repeated what she had said to me and in an instant my world stopped turning. The air around me stood still and at that exact moment a large part of me died.

Omar Mcloud was 7 years younger than me and had lived with my immediate family for many years while growing up. At times when he was a kid, I had to walk him to school. Once I had to talk him out of fighting some kid he wouldn't have stood a chance of beating. I also talked to him about young girls his age and the right way to get their attention. Omar truly was like a little brother to me.

On the night of his death, Omar decided that he and his friends would go out to the Phoenix nightclub, located in downtown Toronto. He was celebrating his 23rd birthday as the clock struck midnight while dancing at the nightclub. Sometime around 3:00 AM, Omar received a phone call from someone on his cellphone. Whoever was on the other end of the call had upset Omar so much that the last thing he told his friends was that he would be back. They questioned where he was going, but Omar stormed off upset, walking up half a block from the nightclub. It was while at this street corner, Omar saw a vehicle that allegedly had at least four people in it. It is believed that Omar knew some, if not all the occupants in the vehicle because it's said that the vehicle pulled over to him and he stuck his head inside one of the open windows. One of the occupants in the vehicle pulled the trigger of a gun and shot Omar point blank in his face. Omar fell to the ground and met his demise on the corner of Sherbourne Street and Wellesley Street, 23 years to the date that he was born.

Confused on what to do and how to handle this, I made my way to Omar's home where his mother, sisters and the rest of my family were in a state of mourning that I had never witnessed before. Their hearts were broken and their minds were in denial. We eventually made our way to the 51 Division the police station closest to where the shooting took place. Two homicide detectives attempted to share their compassion, but it was clear by their weak attempt to show it that this was an unfortunate routine for them, especially in 2005. In the city of Toronto, 2005 was dubbed "the year of the gun". By the end of that year, a city that is ironically nicknamed "Toronto the Good" had 80 murders, 52 of them by guns. It may not sound like a lot compared to many major cities in North America however, consider that just the year prior, the city only saw 27 gun deaths in comparison. Also just one year later, it went back down to 29 homicides by gun. Canada's largest city has seen an increase in murders over the years; however, it is yet to surpass the record of deaths by gun set in 2005. Not to reduce the victims who died that year to just a number, because their lives were much bigger than the number the media tends to put on them, however in case you were wondering, Omar was homicide number 44 of the 52 murdered by guns that year.

As the days went on, the pain and hurt that I felt manifested into a feeling of guilt, believing I could have been out with Omar that night and prevented his death. Of course, his death was impossible to predict, but when you're feeling guilty even the illogical can sound rational enough to resonate more guilt. As much of a struggle the feeling of guilt was for me, the guilt only fed a darker feeling that had cultivated inside of me. A feeling that was truly dark to its inner core and that scares me even when I think back on it today. It was the real and true feeling of revenge.

These thugs took my cousin Omar away from me. The feeling of helplessness rolled through the people I loved the most like an uncontrollable plague, turning everyone's lives upside down and inside out. The more I saw the pain in them, is the more the feeling of vengeance started to eat at my inner being. This feeling of vengeance was new to me personally, at least at this high level, but it definitely was not foreign. See growing up, I would often tread water in the pool of street life in Rexdale. I had dipped my toe in to test the temperature a time or two, but I never swam the depths of that mysterious ocean. I did however hang around enough street cats to know the rules of the game. If they bring a knife, you bring a gun. As I mentioned before, Rexdale, was a very loving and very multicultural neighbourhood in the North West corner of Toronto, but boy was it tough. Especially for a young urban kid. Stats collected by the Toronto Star newspaper indicated that the police who patrolled areas of my neighbourhood had more people criminally charged with violent crimes, such as assault with a weapon and attempted murder than any other police patrolled areas in the city of Toronto (Jim Rankin, 2002). I went to school with friends and acquaintances who used to roll heavy in neighbourhood street gangs; NBC'S (New Born Crips), The Ghetto Boys and MNM'S (Mother Nature's Mistake) just to name a few. I mean, how low do you have to feel about yourself to call yourself Mother Nature's mistake? I recall there was one young drug dealer that I was cool with who sat beside me in high school math class every weekday. One weekend a drug deal that he was involved with went bad when he sold drugs to an undercover cop. Questioning if this narc was truly an officer or if it was a rip off, he took no chances and shot the undercover drug cop in the chest at point-blank range. The officer narrowly but luckily survived and the young man spent most of the rest of his life in jail. I've seen a female student show up to a fight with a school locker combination padlock balled up in her fist to use as a weapon, just to have it backfire and have it used on her to fracture her own skull. I have seen a bunch of gang bangers from a rival school show up at my school to jump and stab a student who "disrespected" one of them during a pick-up basketball game. I held a gun for the first time in the 10th grade when an acquaintance brought one to school and before I hit the age of 18, I knew at least 12 young men who had their lives taken from them due to gun violence. The neighbourhood became so much of a war zone that, while mourners were standing over a casket in a local church, crying over a boy shot to death at the age of 17, his best friend who was standing outside the church, met his own fate. Heartless rival gang bangers pulled up to the funeral and shot the best friend, taking his life, just steps away from where his homeboy laid lifeless. All while the congregation was singing "Amazing Grace" within an earshot of the cold murder. So as you can see, I was surrounded by societal negativity. I survived that hostile social environment and was able to come out unscathed, but not without it leaving a long-lasting impression on me. Although I was able to navigate my way through these years without getting into any serious trouble, I did pick up a lot of lessons from those streets. Some good, some bad and some downright horrible. And now, one of those old downright horrible lessons were showing itself to me in a way that I did not want, but like a moth to a flame, I couldn't resist the urge to fly forward, regardless of the consequence or harm that could come to me. I rationalized that the people who took Omar away would have to pay the ultimate price.

Omar's death put me in a horrible mental state. The funeral was difficult and the progression of the police investigation, or lack thereof was even worse. Every few weeks that would go by, the homicide investigators would finally get around to returning the phone calls of family members looking for answers about the investigation. Through small pieces of information we started to learn details of the case and on occasion, a homicide investigator would call and tell the family that they were expecting to make an arrest fairly soon. That "fairly soon" never came. The ups and downs of the unknowns in the circumstance only added to the family distress and fueled my own fire of vengeance. As a newly hired officer fresh out of the police college, I was at a crossroads. On one side, I had pledged an oath. With crisp and clean lily white gloves on, with one hand on the bible and one hand in the air, to serve and protect the citizens of my city, regardless of whom they were. On the other side of my internal pendulum, I wanted nothing more than to seek and destroy, to watch Omar's killers plead for their lives while I played God standing over them waiting for the exact moment to pull my own trigger. After the soundwaves echoed the fired gunshots, I would watch their bodies move from gasping for air to straight motionless. Their dark souls would finally leave their frame and descend below to the fiery pit of hell. Every day that I walked into work to start my shift, I would suit up in uniform, tighten my duty belt and lastly grab my 9MM Glock handgun. A tool I filled then emptied down range hundreds of times, but only on the firing range. Every day that I would grab this piece of equipment, I would pause and think of how easy it would be to take old faithful home with me and start my own investigation. I could be the judge and jury, but I took a dark satisfaction in imagining being the executioner. I knew that taking my gun home would be easy, as no one would expect to see it until 12 hours later when my next shift started. I mean, can you imagine what the news headlines would say? NEW POLICE RECRUIT KILLS FOUR MEN, USING HIS SERVICE PISTOL TO GET REVENGE ON THE ASSAILANTS WHO KILLED HIS COUSIN. To be honest, I wasn't thinking that far. I couldn't foresee the humiliation this act would have brought to my family, to the police service who hired me, to the fellow officers who wore the uniform and ultimately to myself. After all the hard work and determination to attain a career that I fought so hard for, not even a remnant of this remained in my mind.

I recalled feeling really low and lonely one day. The back and forth within my mind was mentally, physically and spiritually draining. The struggle was real, a true battle within me between love and hate. I wasn't a killer but the pain that was intoxicating my spirit; it blurred my vision in a way that I didn't care about my future. On one specific day, while walking through my police division and buried in my own thundercloud of thought, I abruptly ran into a senior officer. Comparing the two of us, we were polar opposites. He was a white man, about three decades older and outranked me by at least three levels. I intended to say excuse me and keep it moving. After all, still being new, no one knew who I was and no one at that time seemed to care. However, this interaction went differently and was extremely unexpected. As I stepped passed him he said, "Hey Jeff, how you doing?"

I was surprised to hear my name come out of his mouth because I didn't think he knew it. I gave him a hollow, "Fine. Thanks," and remained on my pace.

"Do you have a minute?" he asked me. I stopped walking and turned around. Was I in trouble for something? I wondered. Being fresh out of police college, I was used to senior staff demanding things, not politely asking if I had a minute.

"Hey, I heard what happened to your cousin. I'm truly sorry for your loss," I was again, taken aback by the fact that he knew about my family issues. I didn't tell many people at work. I told my direct supervisor because I had to take some time off for the funeral and family consoling. My supervisor must have told my training coach, because one day when I arrived at work he coldly conveyed his condolences and asked me if I needed time off. I thought he was asking through compassion, but before I could answer, he stated, "Because when you're at work, you need to be focused on the job! If you can't do that, you need to stay at home."

This was the response from my new training officer. One of the first representatives I had in this organization. So because of his sour attitude, I didn't discuss my family issue with anyone. The fact that this senior officer was showing empathy caught me off guard.

"How you holding up?" he asked as he appeared to be settling in for a lengthy conversation. I didn't give him very much. I didn't want to show anyone the rot that was brewing in my heart. After all, at that time I was still battling between the angel on one shoulder and devil on the other. If the devil won, I didn't want anyone to have even an inkling of what my plans were in acting out my revenge. I stood there, silently questioning why I was stopped by this officer who I assumed like the others didn't really care. It soon became quite clear what his intent was. He truly wanted to do nothing more than to encourage me. He started telling me a story of when he was quite young on the job himself; he had a family member gunned down, murdered in cold blood. His family suffered through grief and turmoil, looking for answers that no one would ever give. Just like in my cousin Omar's circumstance, they never caught the murderer who killed his family member. Never brought to justice and never answered for their crime. He also went on to describe the pain he felt, not only because of the unexpected loss of a loved one, not only because it was such a violent way to leave this world, but because at that time like me, he too was a new officer. Since he was now on the side of the law, his family members looked at him to be the solver of this crime. He was new, had no experience and didn't even know how to write a traffic ticket, let alone have the knowledge, skills or abilities to solve a murder. As silly and unreasonable as it sounded, the lack of his competence did not matter to grieving relatives who demanded justice in any form it came in. This senior officer's family demanded answers from anyone wearing a uniform. This now included him, regardless of how fresh out the box his uniform was. My family demanded the same thing. They wanted answers from the police, and so did I, but some of my family expected me to have solutions that I just could not offer. It wasn't even in my power to give. Like the senior officer, part of my pain came from a feeling of hopelessness brought on by family. I had loved ones telling me that I wasn't doing enough. I had family tell me that I should be putting on my uniform and knocking on doors, demanding answers. I think if those relatives looked back and could hear their erratic demands, they would realize how silly and far-out they were in their requests. "Jeff, I don't know where your head is at here, but one thing I know is that you can't let this circumstance eat you up inside. It is going to consume you," he told me this as if he could read my emotions through my expressions. "You need to harness these feelings you have and project them in a way that's going to make you better, the people around you better and your community better." With that, he shook my hand and walked away. I stood there for a moment, frozen and speechless. Since August 15th, the day of Omar's murder, I had been a wreck, emotionally exhausted, conflicted, furious, guilt ridden, hopeless, isolated, depressed and distressed. I had developed an indifference to my new career, my friends, my family, my girlfriend Tasha at that time and everything in life that truly mattered to me. The war of emotions was too much to take and like water pushing on an old dam, my emotions gave way like a flood. Standing in the hallway alone at that moment, I could do nothing else but cry. At that precise moment, alone, I mourned the loss of my little cousin. Nothing else mattered; where I was or who would see me. The emotions I battled with over the last few months left my body through my sobbing. On that day, I started the slow process of my transformation, channeling my anger into a new drive and passion.

When I reflect back on my life, losing Omar in the manner in which I lost him might be one of the ugliest gifts I have ever received. After riding through that emotional rollercoaster and thinking of the pain it produced, I would not wish that kind of anguish on my worst enemy. That mental suffering almost took me to a place of no return. All the joy that I currently have in my life, I would have lost if I continued down that path. It would have been so regrettable. Marrying the love of my life, Tasha in 2007, being present for the birth of my three sons, Jeffery Jr., (lovingly known as J.J.), Chauncey and Karter. Cutting their umbilical cords, changing diapers, taking them to basketball games, helping them work on their jump shot, teaching them to be financially sound, the list goes on. All of those personal blessings I would have missed if I continued to wander down that gruesome path.

As much as my life would not have been the same without receiving these personal blessings, I know that the silver lining or the endowment that I attained from this ugly gift was a mind shifting experience that has lead me down a path of becoming a social activist fighting for change. See I always had the will in me to do good for others, but since Omar's death and surviving such a tough personal trial, I emerged out of my dark place like the ancient Greek mythical firebird. Like a phoenix from the ashes, I rise.

From a place of darkness, I was able to rise and emerge into the leader that I was meant to become.

This young kid from Rexdale, who was barely noticeable, who didn't speak much has materialized into an empowerment speaker, a published author and a social advocate. Instead of seeking revenge on Omar's murderers, I now go into schools, community centres, church groups and social arenas to speak with kids, teens and adults about bettering their lives, finding their passion, targeting for their goals and walking within their purpose.

Long time ago, I came to terms with the fact that I could not stop Omar's murder. Seeking revenge would have continued the vicious cycle in the community. However, what I could do and what I have been continuously doing is giving hope to kids who've grown up surrounded by drugs, poverty, gangs and desperation. For youth raised with no father in the home and a mother who is too busy working to notice or care. To young people forced to make grown up decisions that ultimately affect the rest of their lives. For adults who are stuck in neutral and can't seem to find their footing in this world, these are the people I speak life into! Whether giving a motivational speech in front of a large audience, sharing my weekly motivational videos on social media, offering expressions that inspire personal drive on my podcast or through the words I've published through books, EVERYTHING that I do now is to alter people's mindset and drive them towards their purpose. The way I see it, I don't give myself much choice. See, I was reminded by a friend Jelani Daniel, one of the co-authors of this book that it's extremely important to let you, the readers know that for every action there is an equal and opposite reaction. The way this physics lesson of Newton's third law of motion applied to my life was simple; if I had the capability to exhaust all that energy into potentially taking someone's life, then I'd better apply the same level of energy, determination and focus into saving lives. If I had the potential to think death, then it's my absolute duty to speak life!

I recognize that I may not have been able to stop the young men from killing Omar, but maybe… just maybe my words through a motivational talk, my image through social media, my sharing of knowledge through my podcast or my publications through books can make a difference. Just maybe with all these gifts I've been blessed to share into the world, just one, even a fraction of one would meet the ears of a young man who is on the verge of self-destruction or a young woman who lives in a place of disparity and have it plant a seed that ultimately CHANGES THEIR LIFE! It's quite obvious I couldn't prevent Omar's death, but perhaps I can stop the next senseless killing. Perhaps my words can prevent the next teenage pregnancy or my voice can avert the next young kid tempted to join that gang. Perhaps my reasoning can inhibit the next suicide attempt (which has occurred since writing this book) or any one of these God given talents, simply just inspires someone to be great! If even one of these things has occurred, (and I know that it has) I have found my silver lining, my endowment, my phoenix from the ashes… my gratitude in my ugly gift.

What is your ugly gift? What circumstance have you gone through that has been such a burden in your heart or a weight on your shoulders? I know firsthand how difficult it can be to free yourself from the dark thoughts, anger, resentment and really, the list can go on. But I can also show you by being a living example of how life looks from the other side; the side where you recognize and fixate on the silver lining within the ugly gift. When you place yourself in a state of gratitude, all negativity will be forced to stop dead in its tracks. The two simply cannot occupy the same space at the same time. The more time you have for gratitude, the less you have for the negative. Focusing on the gratitude doesn't make your tragedies go away, but what it does is have you concentrate on what you possess, the things that are important and items that matter. For example, someone who has been handed the ugly gift of cancer may find their silver lining in the fact the family has rallied closer to be around them. Someone who lost their job may have a greater opportunity awaiting them. A person who was once suicidal now has the ability to talk someone else out of taking their own life because they have been there themselves. The lessons found in these ugly gifts are endless, but it requires YOU to find the gratitude in these circumstances. Never forget that a diamond forms under pressure. It doesn't emerge beautiful and showroom ready, it has gone years under compression and hardship before it becomes the beautiful stone that's within. I am proof that whatever you are going through, whatever ugly gift has fallen into your lap... YOU CAN GET THROUGH. You WILL get through! For those who are spiritual, in the Bible Romans 8:18 says and I paraphrase, the pain you've been feeling can't compare to the joy that's coming. Whatever you do, don't ever give up! Within the chaos, struggles and despair of your ugly gift know that there is a silver lining waiting just for you. In everything you do, find the gratitude in your circumstances!

PRINCIPLES FROM JEFF'S STORY

PRINCIPLE 1:

There Is Always A Silver Lining In Your Ugly Gift

In every circumstance that you go through in life, there is always a silver lining; a lesson to be learned or an endowment to be had. Always look for it regardless of how difficult your circumstances may be.

PRINCIPLE 2:

Be Patient, It's Going To Get Better

Romans 8:18 - The pain you've been feeling can't compare to the joy that's coming. These words have been promised to you! Never forget that a diamond is formed under pressure, it doesn't emerge beautiful and showroom ready. It has gone years under compression and hardship before it becomes the beautiful stone that's within. Whatever you are going through, know that somewhere within you is the beautiful diamond. Keep striving and whatever you do, DON'T GIVE UP!

PRINCIPLE 3:

Good Advice Can Come From Anyone At Any Time

Sometimes good advice can come from someone who you are not expecting it from, at a time when you are not expecting it. Be open to good and sound advice and use it to better your situation.

PRINCIPLE 4:

Don't Allow Your Past To Dictate Your Future

Despite how difficult of a past you may have grew up in, do not allow that to dictate the decisions you make going forward in life. Your decisions need to be made soundly, even in the most difficult of times.

PRINCIPLE 5:

Find Gratitude

Even in the toughest of times, you can find gratitude. If you can be thankful in the best of times, it then becomes easier to be thankful on the days that you find it hard even to get out of bed. As tough as you have it, someone always has it more difficult. It doesn't belittle what you are going through, but it helps you to put things into perspective. When you place yourself in a state of gratitude, all negativity will be forced to stop dead in its tracks. The two simply cannot occupy the same space at the same time.

PRINCIPLE 6:

Never Underestimate The Impact Your Story Can Have On Someone Else's LIfe

Because of the hurt and pain that you may have been though in your life, you can use your story to teach others. There are people out there who are going through exactly what you went through. You have the ability to teach, to inspire and to transform lives!

JEFF A.D. MARTIN

As a result of Jeff A.D. Martin's work as an empowerment speaker, author of a critically acclaimed children's book, the face of exceedingly shared social media motivational videos and host of a globally downloaded podcast, Jeff has inspired many to step through their biggest fears, pursue their most unnerving passions and find their life's purpose. Jeff is an award winning international public speaking contest winner and simply wants to see people step into their greatness!

Website: Jeffadmartin.com

Social media: @jeffadmartin

CHAPTER FIVE

CIRCUMSTANCES DO NOT DICTATE DESTINY
BY JELANI DANIELS

"Overcoming adversity and difficult situations and staying on the right path. Knowing to have faith in your growth. The most important aspect is self-reliance - becoming the master of your own destiny."

The journey I have endeavored throughout my life can be compared to the human body- the human body utilizes all its parts to work together in harmony, ensuring a seamless function.

The environments, the situations, the people and all the setbacks endured worked together to build a mosaic; a template to sustain life and to carry out my journey. You will see throughout my story that momentary excitement and rewards were alluring but led to downfalls. I want to invite you to understand my origins and in the end, better understand the human journey that is intrinsic to so many of us.

Nevis, a sun-kissed Caribbean country with a population of 19,000 was my birthplace. Each morning I would converse with fellow students, parents and teachers on my way to school. Discipline was sanctioned from the local community on children until the age of 10; this taught me respect and mental restraint. As I evolved, so did my understanding of the world and how to better at future attempts of discipline. This set the stage for further exploits, while still maintaining an understanding of respect for my elders – which ultimately implemented a foundation for my life of how to carry out planned movements for necessary outcomes all while being aware.

Our community consisted of people, real bodies and lives, not televisions and the conventional media channels Westernized society is accustomed to. This taught me and I continue to teach my children, the value of connection and ownership in your community.

When positivity and ownership conquer negativity, endless doors open and the first window that opened was on a late-night plane to Toronto Pearson International Airport in Canada. The beaming airport lit up my mind- the colours were spectacular and all of the lights were remarkable. Seeing the taxi merge on the highway fascinated me and made my mind travel alongside the following traffic. Nevis was a land of modesty, barely entertaining 20 cars at a time, devoid of a highway.

The individuality of peers was conflicting. From a young age, Nevis was a community unit and the colder distance, especially in testing and regular schoolwork was all novel. Such differences being highlighted allowed me insight into my own true self, a reflection I never had the chance to have previously- my value was never highlighted in my previous life, but now it was on the main stage and I had to defend it.

Understanding my value was essential to getting through the growing pains of bullies, peer pressure and other pressures that accompany life's tests- when you know your intrinsic value, nothing can take it away but alongside such confidence, you may face a war with yourself. Questioning your next move and clouded judgment eventually creates cracks in your armor. As mine surfaced, mediocre grades and an air of indifference ensued, departing from the responsibilities I once held close.

Entering adulthood, I played a strong move towards being myself rather than carrying out the jaded view of painful restraint- I wanted to be the best version of Jelani Daniel. There always were and always will be people and systems vying on the negative side of possibility and like many teens, I was sold the fleeting negative view.

After three years of Canadian living, I found myself rebelling against my mother. An individualist view led to reckless nights of disobeying orders, staying at friend's houses and escaping myself through momentary relief- it made me feel alive. My close friends, my pack, consisted of a well-rounded group of diverse minds. We shared a neighbourhood but maintained unique minds that drifted between teenage dreams and the Wall Street News. No topic was off-limits which led to a sense of euphoria. We were figuring out who we were in the prime years of our lives, living a young life full of uncertainty and some deceit to find a greater meaning we never wanted before.

Petty theft led to excitement and thrills, even if I did not take part. I was learning about what was taken, the car parts. It led to interesting conversation and my eventual hobby and lifeline later in life- cars. Petty theft led to auto theft and while I watched on the sidelines, my support system stayed close to me to keep my path clear of criminality. For such support, I always maintained intense gratitude. My mother, a hard worker always ensured I had all that I needed and kept me emotionally warm during the seasons of change my life endured. To hurt her would hurt me, so I maintained the discipline taught by my community and avoided the criminal life that was lavishly waved in my face; it was for her and all those that supported me.

My support system encouraged my growth

The support of my friends and family taught me to unlock my highest potential and accepted me unconditionally because they knew my heart. Without a great support system, toxic lifestyles can become alluring. Thankfully, I could recognize and avoid toxic relationships, but still maintain friendships. Although not directly linked to the crimes themselves I provided buyers, sellers and vice versa- my duty during high school and within my neighborhood was that of the middle-man.

Their callous lifestyle and my recognized status started to normalize and eventually, full-fledged "chop shops" were managed effectively by youth as young as 17-years-old. The commercial growth of breaking down car parts, often servicing five cars at a time, made me realize at my young age, the undervalued intelligence of the youth, which has carried over to my current timeline.

As we aged, so did the severity of the actions we were engaged in. Stories about running from police actualized and the story we told ourselves over the years reaped heavy consequences. Fights broke out, criminality in larger volumes ensued, injuries were assessed and stolen items disappeared- we were losing control. Tension was an undercurrent to all aspects of my life, all interactions, making me reminisce on my simple life before on the island. I saw so many tragic stories on the rare television Sunday mornings and now I was caught up in the lifestyle that seemed so surreal. It was really happening to me- I was becoming the stories I watched as a child on the news.

My reality became tense. I went from the small island boy that would watch these stories every Sunday, to living in it, front and center. During this time, I lost one of my best friends, Anthony aka "B". I came to know of his murder in a way that I will never forget.

The Day You See The Consequence Of Your Decisions Is A Day You'll Never Forget

Anthony, also known as "B", who was one of my best friends, was shot and murdered. I found out all the details on the morning news. His blue Nike sneakers showed up on the screen and all I remember is feeling a sense of loss and reality struck again. Anthony was a local Toronto furniture store owner, a unique and caring friend and someone who I formed a strong bond with. He was a large part of my world and now he was gone. Revenge was a focal theme in my life and the life of my friends thereafter, it was marked by an urge to murder the person who had murdered my friend, but this would only perpetuate an already broken cycle in my neighborhood. My mother reminded me time and time again of the pain it would cause to another family, another group of friends.

Living in Parkdale his fate was subjective, especially in the early 1990s, shifting my life view to one ensnared in danger. There was a rampant crack scene and many peers were present with ulterior, dangerous motives – stickups and petty theft were common. One night, a knife was held to my chest and my money was taken, this reminded me how freakishly close death was in my neighborhood. It left a stain on my perception of Parkdale.

After losing one of my closest friends, I realized the importance of making your mind an ally; without a strong relationship with yourself, you are depriving yourself of prosperity. Such significance applied to your very being, allows you to silence the chaos of all that stands in your way and appear graceful in the face of uncertainty. I was alive and I was thankful. I had lost someone very important but maintained so many others I loved; I was fortunate even after loss.

You Need To Love Yourself To Save Yourself

No person has the right to take the life of another and equally, you have no right to take away your life with thoughts of hate and small thinking. Calming those in the midst of crisis and vengeance saved the targets of such scorn. The lives of those who wanted revenge were calmed and in the end, love made the difference.

Criminality is not innate to black men and women. It is not our job to hate, it is our right to love and it is my right to help you understand the importance of eradicating such stigma. A race is not predisposed to crime and violence, crime and violence stand alongside inner battles and false storytelling. We are not the negative story we have been told we are. Most killings occur due to retaliation. It is a choice and you have the right to make different choices.

Thinking back, what stopped me from actively carrying out retaliation was my mother's love, support and the desire for freedom- freedom from hatred and the freedom to enjoy life outside of prison. A momentary escalation to mitigate an inner conflict was not resolve at all; it's the essence of faulty storytelling about how to resolve conflicts within one's self. It was a cowardly approach to life, true strength lay in forgiveness and celebrating his life, not regretting his last day- that would demote his legacy.

What We Think About Brings Us Energy Or Removes Our Energy

We can either prepare to feel low and worthless, a common feeling for most people, or we can choose to use the strength that we have developed and emit our energy elsewhere. Whichever one we choose, it consumes us and either deviates or propels us towards our goals. When we are patient with ourselves, we stop at the "should haves" and start looking forward to undiscovered truths and new terrain. Time is your fuel for discovery and when you discover, you empower yourself and others further. When you pair time with love, you get positive energy to conquer change and grow.

My roots, my positive surroundings and my full heart have propelled me; leading me to become an Amazon bestselling author, an author of two books and a motivational life coach. Although my feats are wonderful, my biggest accomplishment by far is being a loving father to three amazing children (Tamia, Roman and [super] Nova) and husband to my loving wife Judi. Thank you for always standing by my side.

Seeing people reach their full potential over time is my mission and has been a work in progress since my youth. With the release of my books and speaking publicly, it has been a dream come true. As a visible minority, I pieced instances of insight, deliberation and the will to overcome adversity to make such life lessons into digestible snippets for everybody to read on their personal journey, regardless of background. Such writings allow an equal playing field with other acclaimed authors since words cannot bear race- language is an equal learning tool, and the Forward March movement allows for forward propulsion no matter your age, class, race or gender. It is our duty as humans to help one another, a commitment so strong that it cannot be bought or sold and one that we should continue to pursue despite the many objections or roadblocks we will face. As documented earlier, roadblocks are merely lessons disguised as disappointment.

Being at a point in my life where I can share my knowledge, not merely from speculation, but from far-reaching experience is pivotal to me and everyone I speak to. At a young age, we often listen to others around us to learn about ourselves, but as we grow, such information can detract us from who we are and who we are meant to be. It took me a number of years, through hard work and adversity, to understand that my life and my calling are unique to me, as yours is to you- do not let anyone take away what is so purposefully yours.

When We Can Understand Ourselves, We Can Craft A Unique Identity That Keeps Us On The Right Track

As I grew and matured, there were valuable lessons to be learned and one came quite recently when writing my first book; I learned how to be vulnerable. The walls we use to keep ourselves safe can sometimes block out what we need to become great. So by letting down some of my defenses, I was able to instill in myself and hopefully others, a feeling of confidence in motion.

Throughout the writing process, there were a number of different perspectives on how I should write, what was written and what should be different. Some thoughts came in the form of congratulations, others in the form of criticism and some as silence; signifying diversity even when presenting new facets of our being. When you "level up" not everyone will understand or relate to what you present, but you have a unique opportunity to bring a new perspective to the lives of others if you believe in yourself.

Developing new quotes, ideas and partnerships gave a unique light to everything I did. Granting access to greater and greater opportunities and most importantly, greater and greater friends. The friends along the way, my loving family and my roots instilled the importance of staying on track in somewhat troubling times.

No matter your race, status, or income you are deserving of what lies on the other side of your fear.

Social media and television may paint a perfect picture for others in your area, but such snapshots are not reality. We are often discouraged from seeing the real person behind the scenes.

Recognizing The Value of Illusions Is Priceless

When we can sit still, sit with ourselves and understand all that makes up our being, it allows for a certain flexibility in life so few can compete with because it's not a competition with anyone but ourselves. Train yourself to beat the odds, to stand up each morning with purpose without the sway of unnecessary illusions outlined in media outlets. Know yourself and present it to the world with pride- you deserve to be more than you fear you cannot become.

We cannot measure our stories on the stories of others

As leaders, we become teachers, influencers and community members for future generations, equipping them so they can positively tap into their greatest potential. Globalization, profiteering, violence and racism; these are not the full picture of your story. Your value, your future is not held hostage based on certain life events. We have the amazing opportunity to reinvent ourselves over and over according to our circumstances and the resilience lies in understanding your personal value.

Opportunity is a marvellous tool that does not fade or run out, if anything, it is more abundant than ever with social media and the internet at our fingertips; how blessed we are. Learning is endless, freedom is a reality and you have the right to reach your highest potential- never let false stories tell you otherwise. Humans have the ability to adapt and imagine. You have the ability to unleash your full potential, no matter your race.

We Are All Equal In The Eye Of Opportunity

Opportunity is not elusive, it is all around us, but we have to put ourselves out there in order to catch a glimpse of it. As a young child, I pursued freedom and the ability to learn and grow. As I grew, I craved the opportunity to help others reach their dreams. Simply craving a successful ending was not enough, I had to work long hours, network excessively, write and edit. Then make time for other work, family and a social life. The balance was a struggle, but in the end, it all boiled down to meeting different people on different journeys seeking the same opportunity; to be their best selves.

Opportunity may seem impossible, but we all have the ability to make a lucky break or speak to the one person who will change our life with a single connection. Everyone has struggles, some more than others, but what makes the difference is not only the belief that opportunity is present but the action that puts the belief into motion. When you believe you have the opportunity to accomplish all your wildest dreams, you have already taken the first step. Quitting my day job and writing a book was mine – I got a lot of pushback, but after the pushback came massive rewards. You have the ability to be more than you could ever imagine, but you have to step outside of what you know, meet people you've never met and maintain a level of courage that may seem surreal, but is within you. You have the courage to win.

Pursue your greatest fears and leave no stone unturned. Reflect and never forget; you are destined to be the greatest version of yourself.

PRINCIPLES FROM JELANI'S STORY

PRINCIPLE 1:

Your Unique Story

My story encompasses an original path that was presented to me and it all started with believing I had the tools to make my visions a reality - no one else held the answer. In life, we are fortunate to have vision, but to follow through with such ambitions takes great courage and self-belief, despite pushback from those around you. There will be events and adversity, but as with any great story, it takes great strides to become your own hero.

PRINCIPLE 2:

Kindness As A Tool

Throughout my life, kindness has been a tool that has expanded my horizons and brought my visions to a realistic setting. Without self-care, compassion for others and empathy when hearing of extreme hardships, inspiration would have been scarce in my lifetime. By understanding and loving myself and others, opportunities were presented because a new point of view opened up. Negativity gives us a narrow scope of what life entails, but when you open your heart, the world is your playground.

PRINCIPLE 3:

The Most Important Takeaway

The most important takeaway is overcoming adversity and difficult situations and staying on the right path. This comes from knowing yourself and having faith in your growth. With personal growth, the most important aspect to maintain is self-reliance. Self-reliance allows you to become the master of your own destiny and look back on the roots that have sewn your path. On your path, it is important to remember that your circumstances do not dictate your destiny. If anything, they lend a helping hand to accomplishing more than you thought possible by providing a viable source of fuel to carry out your highest potential.

JELANI DANIEL

As an avid entrepreneur for the past 14 years, and the voice of mastery, Jelani has reached and encouraged large audiences, making it to the Amazon Best Sellers list, lending an empowering voice to all generations. With his wife and three lovely children by his side, Jelani has become a well-known speaker throughout his community and global audiences. "Forward March", a movement founded by Jelani, stipulates the importance of being our best selves and helping one another no matter our race, gender, income or status. As he continues his mission, Jelani's influence is both heard and felt; he is the voice of mastering our greatest destiny.

Website: Jelanidaniel.ca

CHAPTER SIX

RESPONSE VS. REACTION

By Randell Adjei

By the time I was twelve years old, I was arrested on three separate occasions for robbery, failure to comply and assault. I was a juvenile delinquent who was in and out of court and detention centres. In middle school, my principal said I was the worst student she ever had in thirty-one years in the education system. I was an angry child who verbally and even physically fought both my parents on separate occasions. In my opinion, I wasn't a bad kid, I just made some bad decisions and hung out with friends who pressured me into things I knew were wrong. I stole from people because I didn't grow up having much. I got into many fights because I carried some serious anger in my heart.

In just six years, I went from a troubled child to a School Council President, Ontario Scholar and Valedictorian of my high school graduating class. I graduated with four awards and a scholarship. Receiving all those awards and becoming Valedictorian of my class was one of the most pivotal moments of my life. It was life changing. I remember standing on stage, speaking to the crowd as I spotted my proud mother in the audience. She was teary eyed and beaming with a beautiful smile. My mother was there with me 99 out of the 100 court dates I had. She would work an eight-hour shift from midnight to 8am and she would painfully come to court at 9am to support me. She wasn't able to make it to one court date I had because her arthritis was just too painful one day. She was the only one who still believed in me and supported me through the adversity. It was my mom who continued loving me as a troubled twelve-year-old and seen me through my graduation; when everyone else had written me off as a lost cause.

It was August 3rd, 2009; I had just graduated high school and was preparing for my first year in university. Summer was ending and my friends and I were all moving into different phases of our lives, so we wanted to party and celebrate. That day I bought myself a new chain with some of the money I saved up working all summer. It was a Jesus piece, shimmering with yellow gold and diamonds surrounding the face of Christ. I had two chains that night but decided to let my friend Jay wear one to evade too much attention. We all came dressed to impress. We drove thirty minutes to Downtown Toronto's club district and we had an amazing time at the party. The party ended around 3am and we were hanging out in front of the club catching up with some old friends enjoying the post party vibe. In the blink of an eye, we heard a round of gunshots blasting in the night's sky. Immediately, hundreds of people started running for safety. It was chaos. The shots were loud and scary. None of us knew where the shots were coming from so we decided to stay put and wait for the chaos to end. I remember looking at my friends and just thinking, damn, it was all good just a minute ago. Shortly after the gunshots seemed to have ended, Jay received a call from some other friends at a nearby party. They said that they were the ones shooting. They explained that they were just having fun shooting randomly in the air. They asked us to come and meet up with them at a nearby parking lot. They were friends we knew well and we felt it was safe to go and meet with them despite the circumstances. Because I knew how dangerous the club scene could be, I tucked my chain in my polo shirt to avoid attention as we started walking towards them.

There was only Jay, his cousin Alex and me. By this time, most people in the area already moved from the scene but a good number were still around. On our way there, I was responding to some text messages on my cell phone while Jay and Alex were walking a few feet in front of me. They were in a deep conversation and I was looking at my phone when I heard some voices behind us. I turned around and saw a group walking towards us. I didn't think much of it; they were far enough away that I couldn't really foresee what happened next. I went back to texting, but suddenly a weird feeling in the pit of my stomach emerged. I turned around and saw the same group of guys. Now I could see that they were all dressed in black hoodies and actually had them over their heads and were walking suspiciously fast towards us. The weird feeling in the pit of my stomach heightened.

I turned back and told Jay and Alex that something was wrong; they turned around to look behind them. They were so into their conversation that they didn't think much of it, "Don't worry Randell, we're good." replied Jay and we kept walking. I didn't feel right so I put my phone in my pocket and kept my head forward walking as fast as I could. The third time I turned around I heard the sound of a switchblade slicing through the air as it opened. Within seconds, I was surrounded by seven angry guys and had a sharp knife pointing at my chest. I felt hands digging through my pockets. My hat was taken off my head and there was a tall guy standing there holding the knife to my chest examining me. His eyes fixed on my face and neck. Surrounded, scared and shocked, I remember looking past him to the sky and thinking, "God, why me?" It was one of the most terrifying moments of my life. They were yelling and screaming at me to stay still. Each of them had a knife in their hand. All I saw were several knives pointing towards me and guys in hoodies who were ready to do something if I made the wrong move. I didn't know how this was going to turn out. Was this just a robbery or the last scene of my life? The fact that someone else held my fate in their hands both angered and scared me. I started thinking about my mom and the potential of never seeing her again. I thought about my friends and wondered if I would ever have the chance to tell them this story. That's when I started worrying about Jay and Alex. For a moment, my mind went blank and I forgot I was even with them. I frantically looked around and just a bit ahead of me, I saw Alex on the floor. He was getting kicked and stomped on mercilessly by the set of hoodlums who left me to rob him. Alex's hands and arms were sheltering him from some of the blows.

It was hard to watch. Then I turned slowly to my right and saw Jay running desperately for his life. Chased by his own group of goons in all black with knives in hand. They were ripping at his shirt and they pulled the chain I had loaned him that night off his neck. I watched it break as one of the guys pocketed it. It was like a movie; Jay kept fighting to break free. I made some rough calculations, there were about twenty gangsters attacking the three of us in total. I tried to keep my eyes on the situation but the feeling of the knife to my chest brought me back to the present moment that my life was also in serious danger. I was angry, there was nothing I could do at that moment to help my friends or myself. I was furious, I was scared, I was helpless and I was just trying not to die.

They emptied everything from my pockets. Once the group that surrounded me realized I had nothing else on me, most of the guys joined the chase to catch Jay who was still fighting to break free. There was only the tall slender guy left, knife still to my chest. He was hoodied up so I really couldn't see his face which made it that much scarier. I was nervous, angry and scared all at the same time. I thought to run but I didn't know if he had a gun, if he did, he may have reacted and shot me in my back. At this point, I only had my chain, the clothes on my back and my life left. My brain told me not to run but I felt that in order to survive I had to because I didn't know who the robber was, I just couldn't take the chance.

So, I stood there scared wondering why he stuck around and what he wanted from me. It felt like an eternity. During near death experiences, it's as if time freezes. I was certainly frozen at that moment unable to run with my life essentially in another man's hands. After what seemed like forever, he started examining my neck. It was almost as if he knew all along when he quickly reached under the collar of my shirt and snatched the Jesus piece without hesitation. That situation was one of the most dreadful I've ever gone through. I remember him pulling it off my neck when for a split second the Jesus piece was facing me. I looked at the face of Christ on my chain as it disappeared forever.

After that, I stood there still feeling scared, but now confused about what to do. After he had taken the chain, I realized they took everything from me and I had nothing else in my possession to offer. If it really was just a robbery, I wasn't going to stand there to have my life taken too. Although I didn't know whether he had a gun on him, my intuition at that time strongly suggested I run to get to a safer location. My life was all I had at that point and I wasn't willing to lose it just 26 days before my 18th birthday. I wasn't going to be another statistic, another black boy who wouldn't make it to see 25. I ran because my life really did depend on it. I ran and ran. I feared getting shot in my back if this guy really did have a gun. Fortunately, I wasn't shot. I ran a few yards before seeing another group of guys walking towards the scene. These guys seemed really concerned about what was happening. They were so fashionably dressed and I felt I could trust them by their demeanor so I hysterically explained the situation. I started yelling and crying as I explained to them I had been robbed and needed their help. "What happened? What happened!?" they asked. "I just got robbed and I really really need your help to get my stuff back," I exclaimed. They looked at each other and paused a moment. "Please guys, I really need your help. These guys over there just took everything from me," I yelled. Almost like a scene out of a movie, I just felt the energy shift. I felt their hands grabbing my arms, preventing me from moving my limbs. I froze in a split second of confusion and looked to the 3am night sky again and I heard a voice within say, "Randell, we are not going to die today." Can you imagine the only group of people on the street were not looking to help me but to take advantage of a man who's already down? They were looking to rob an already robbed man. It took every cell in my body to fight this group of guys off me. I was so confused as to what they intended to do. To this day, this part of the story still baffles me. I just remember breaking free only to have another arm grab me again and again. In the midst of this, I got a glimpse in my periphery and seen the same tall, hooded guy who had taken my chain just a few yards away. As I broke free from this second set of men, the tall chain snatcher moved in again and I remember seeing him lunging with the knife, attempting to stab me.

To this day, I have no idea how, but I got away. I broke free for a moment long enough before another hand could grasp me. I started running, injured, disheveled, chainless and with only one shoe on. I ran until I found myself in front of the club that I was initially partying in just an hour earlier and saw a police officer casually standing outside their car. I screamed at the officer hysterically. "Why didn't you save me?! What are you even good for? I almost died and here you are chilling by your car!?" I was yelling loud and the officer clearly seeing I was distressed, tried to calm me down but I was passed that point.

Before I could finish yelling and unleashing a tirade of bad words, I felt arms bear hug me and lift me off the ground. I was fighting back enraged. What next? I thought. I could see the officer's face confused. Then I heard a voice in my ear telling me to calm down before I got arrested. It was my friend Richie's voice. Richie a good friend of mine who I played basketball with in high school was coincidentally out partying too. He literally brought me to the other side of the street where I was able to calm down a little bit. When he finally put me down, I was a bit calmer but still shocked by what had taken place. Richie was looking me up and down. He asked me what happened and then he interrupted before I could finish and said, "Randell, you're bleeding bro."

At that moment, I thought, man how can these guys be so cruel to take all my stuff then try to take my life after? I looked down to my fingertips and realized I was bleeding from my elbow. Richie made a few calls to some of our friends he was partying with and within a few minutes, we walked over to go meet with them. I couldn't find Jay or Alex and I was starting to get worried. When the friends that Ritchie called exited the club, I wildly explained what had happened but they were so high and drunk that they could care less. They didn't care to console me or even take me to the hospital. One of my friends I had known since I was ten was among that group. I was hurt by how apathetic he was about the situation. Word got around about what happened to me and about five minutes later a car pulled up and I jumped in and headed for the hospital. Before going to the hospital, we circled the area looking for Jay and Alex. When we didn't see them, we went looking for my missing shoe and maybe see if we could find these guys who robbed me. We found no signs of Jay and Alex, no shoe and no one that matched the description.

On our way to the hospital, I started thinking about the series of unfortunate events- of being at the wrong place at the wrong time. Then I pondered if we had only gotten to our friends with guns this may not have happened. If we got to them and had a way to defend ourselves- we wouldn't have been robbed. I was stuck in my mind but my body was not speaking to me, the adrenaline had settled down a bit and I could feel the sharp pain in my elbow from the stab wound. I also felt a sharp sensation in my back. I turned to my friend who was with me in the backseat and asked him if he saw any blood on the back of my shirt. Of course, it was dark and he couldn't see the blood that covered the left side of my shirt. So I took my shirt off and touched the part of my back where I felt a sharp and uncomfortable sensation. I pulled my hand back and felt a wet and cold liquid in my hands. That's when I realized I also got stabbed in my back. We rushed to the hospital Emergency. I waited almost an hour before Alex and Jay walked in with some scratches but no significant damage. I almost cried. I was so relieved that they were okay but even more relieved that they came to the hospital to make sure I was good and grateful that they came after hearing what happened. When I was called to see the doctor, I took off my shirt and looked at the left side discovering six holes in my purple blood-stained shirt. I noticed there were holes in the shirt that miraculously didn't puncture my left side; just a minor poke from the tip of the knife that had no significant damage. This is when I truly understood how close I was to losing my life. I received stitches on my left elbow and my upper left back just under my shoulder blade. After lying to the doctor about what happened, I left the room and I was relieved to find the waiting room was full of my friends, at least the ones who truly cared for me, waiting for me with water, sandals and hugs. Right then and there I knew what the definition of true friendship meant.

In the days that followed, I had friends who called me upset about what happened. Some felt bad and offered their condolences. Some called and said they were ready to retaliate on my behalf.

Knowing these guys as well as I did, I knew how far they would go for me. Through word on the street, I learned that the goons who mugged me were going up and down the streets that night robbing dozens of people before and after my attack. My friends made calls and were able to get some crucial information about who they were. Surprisingly, they even found out what neighbourhood they came from and where they were going to be a few days later. My friends were ready to make these guys pay for violating and I was all for it at first. I didn't go home that night or the following day. When I finally got home, I had to lie to my mom about getting robbed and stabbed, too afraid to tell her the truth that I almost died a couple nights before. I lied and told her I got into a fight and fell down and got cut by glass.

I started thinking about these guys who robbed and stabbed me and thought what good would come if I retaliated and they died? Or if one of my friends actually went through with the retaliation and lost his life? Or if I lost mine? When I really thought about it, it wasn't worth the trouble of losing my life or ending up in jail. When I took a moment to be alone and think about the situation, I felt bad for the guys who did what they did to me. I felt bad for them because they must have really been broken to do what they did to me. No happy person walks around planning to rob and stab innocent people. I used to hang out with some guys who did the exact same things these guys did to me. I started thinking, what made my attackers so broken that they had to do what they did to me? My friends and my attackers were actually two sides of the same coin. When I thought about my friends at the time who were involved in these kinds of crimes, I realized that they were all hurting in silence. These were the guys who would often come to me in secrecy to tell me about their problems. Many of them spoke to me about not having their father's in their lives. Not really getting the love and attention, they wanted because their moms were busy working all day and were too tired to give them the love they needed. I started reflecting on the fact that my attackers weren't too different from my own friends at the time. That maybe they too were going through the same issues my friends opened up to me about. After all, they say hurt people hurt people. If these guys were so hurt to do what they did to me, and my friends were so hurt they wanted to kill some strangers on my behalf, then there had to be something I could do to help.

If I had gone through with retaliating, I would only be reacting with the same energy my attackers had put on me. I discovered that reacting and responding are two very different things that I eventually learned to come to grips with. Reacting is a form of retaliating with the same energy initiated. Responding is taking progressive action towards a resolution. I started looking inward. Rather than blaming life or the guys who hurt me, I really started asking myself why this happened to me. Many people have lost their lives to senseless violence, I was fortunate enough to walk away with my life and I am eternally grateful. I felt like this situation happened to me for a reason. I knew within, that I had a deeper purpose. That if I was meant to die that night, I would have. But I didn't and it was like a rebirth process of realizing I still had work to do here on earth. This is when I started to go to work on myself. I began my journey of introspection and discovered some amazing takeaways from the situation that almost took my life.

It took a while before I thought this way but I eventually accepted the situation knowing I couldn't do anything to change what had already happened. At that time I looked at my stab wounds and realized they weren't going anywhere. Today, I still have the scars present as a gentle reminder that the pain I felt emotionally, physically and mentally was not going to go away through retaliation, anger or feeling sorry for myself. I accepted what had happened and began thinking about how I wanted to respond moving forward. I did a lot of internal work in the years that followed. I spent a lot of time learning about myself and discovering where I wanted to be. I spent a lot of time alone, asking myself some introspective questions about my mortality and what I wanted to do with this second chance at life I was given. I was reading self-help books and mentoring in my community. I started talking to mentors more and began deeply exploring my passions. I started university exactly 30 days after the stabbing. During this time, I also accepted that my friends who were too drunk and high to help me in my time of dire need were not my friends at all and I made the choice to cut them off. They weren't going to get me where I needed to go so I had to accept this hard truth and move on. Cutting off those friends was an amazing decision because I no longer felt I had to be someone I wasn't to fit into their circle. I also accepted the fact that whatever I chose to do from that moment forward was going to be up to me in relation to where I wanted to go. This is where I realized what happened moving forward was based on my responsibility - my ability to respond.

Poetry has always been an art I have used to express my feelings. I find poetry to be an amazing outlet for people going through difficult times or as a form of cathartic practice. I used poetry as a way to continue my healing process. During this internal work, I started thinking about how I could share my experiences with others. When I thought about my former friends and my attackers that night, I realized that most people who go through adversity don't have a community or a place to express their pain and heal. When people aren't able to safely express pain and trauma, it festers and can lead to self-doubt, addiction, violence and many other debilitating things. So, I spent some time talking to my friends and peers about what they would like to see in the community and how something like this could benefit them. I got some amazing feedback. Afterwards, I went to work on my execution.

It took about four months of planning, meeting with friends and new people before the idea fully formed. During that time, I spoke to some of my friends and family about what I wanted to do. Some were encouraging while other family members and close friends didn't understand it or thought it was a waste of my time. It hurt to hear some of the negative feedback especially from my parents who didn't agree with it at first because they had a different vision for my life, but I knew the vision was mine, not theirs to see.

My vision was to start a movement; a community-based initiative that offered a safe and inclusive space for youth to express, connect and heal.

At first, it started as just a weekly open mic platform for youth and artists to come and share their challenging experiences through performance art (spoken word poetry, music, dance, hip-hop). It started as a program that would inspire and uplift in hopes of building a community that was willing to listen and offer support so that more people would find the courage to share their pain and experiences. Although there were many hurdles in making the vision come to life, on April 16th, 2012 the movement was born. The movement is called R.I.S.E. (Reaching Intelligent Souls Everywhere) and we hosted our very first R.I.S.E. event in Scarborough, Ontario, Canada starting with 23 people at our first event. Over time, it quickly grew to 40 and 50 people on a weekly basis. Each week new faces joined us with hopes of sharing their stories, their talents or finding a community they could belong to. On July 16th, 2012, 90 people attended our show. The program was amazing and I remember feeling a sense of fulfillment that I, someone who almost lost his life almost three years prior was creating such amazing experiences for so many others.

Shortly after the show, two young girls broke news of a shooting at a community barbeque just 10 minutes away, in a tough neighbourhood named Danzig that I frequented while growing up. To this day, the Danzig shooting is reported to be one of the worst in Canadian history, 25 people were shot and two young people lost their lives that night. The girls proceeded to tell me that they planned on going to the barbeque but decided to come to R.I.S.E. because they knew it was a safe place to be. They were shocked by what happened but also glad they decided to come to R.I.S.E. At this moment, I knew what I started was divine intervention, a safe haven for youth in Toronto. I knew that R.I.S.E. had to continue growing and reaching more people across the Greater Toronto Area. So, every Monday for the rest of that year we continued growing, eventually gaining numbers of 100 each week and often at capacity. On our last event in 2012, word got around and 223 people showed up. By the end of that night, I cried, remembering that I almost never made it to see my vision manifest. Since its inception in 2012, R.I.S.E. has hosted over 350 events and has gathered over 30,000 people at our shows. The event has opened up opportunities for many of those artists including myself to give speeches, workshops and speak at school assemblies in attempts to inspire youth to evolve. R.I.S.E. has helped build hundreds of leaders, inspired people to start their own businesses and has given thousands a platform to find and express their voice. To this date, R.I.S.E. has won more than 15 awards including the Vital Ideas and Vital Youth awards from the Toronto Foundation and has been funded by the municipal and provincial government.

I have also received numerous awards in my name for my work including the Local Hero Award from NOW Magazine and the 2015 Torontonian of the Year by the Canadian Broadcasting Channel, a national TV station.

I've had the opportunity to share stages with celebrities and powerful influencers across the globe. I cannot count the thousands of people that have expressed gratitude for what I was able to start and the impact it has had on them to be better and do better in the world. I attribute their gratitude to the amazing journey I have had in getting to this place. As weird and maybe surprising as it may sound to you, I am thankful to my attackers because they helped me find purpose in my life by nearly taking it.

What I am about to share below is a culmination of the powerful lessons I learned and the wisdom I was able to put into practice after the incident.

ACCEPTANCE: I believe it is important for us to take

time to heal from our wounds. An integral aspect of the healing journey is accepting the current situation as it is instead of trying to fight for what we think should happen.

RESPONSIBILITY: Simply put it is our ability to respond effectively to every situation. That response makes room for personal growth and wisdom to bear its fruits.

Finding the seeds of opportunity in every adversity: In every situation, there is a learning opportunity. It's all about our perspective though. We can choose to see a situation as harmful or "bad" based on our perspective. I believe it's important to note that "good" and "bad" are subjective.

In sharing this story, I hope that you can look at your life and see what hardships or adversities have shaped you. Despite the fact that time may have passed, and you may have "moved on" there may be more for you to learn and take from the experience. Have you accepted the things that life has thrown at you? If you have, great. However, for most people who haven't fully accepted that thing I spoke about earlier, that thing makes them angry or holds them back from being their best self.

I pray that my story will allow you to see that you haven't fully accepted the situation and how by accepting you can move on and forgive yourself or the person who may have caused your pain. By accepting, we are taking responsibility for what has happened to us and we are opening up our hearts to more pleasurable and powerful experiences.

What have you learned from that adversity or hardship? What can you learn? How can it help you grow better, wiser?

None of us are born exempt from struggle and pain but we are born with the consciousness to persevere and overcome. We all have the capacity to become the people we so desperately desire to be. We just have to look deep within ourselves, sit alone with ourselves and ask some deep questions that will allow us to heal and overcome our trauma and pain.

By accepting, taking responsibility and finding the seeds of opportunity in our hardships, we are transcending the curse of judging and being the victims of circumstances designed for us to triumph. I hope this story has provided you with some insightful answers and things to consider about how to become the best we were meant to become. This is a short poem I wrote as a reminder of where I have been and where I am now.

I am not my struggles

I am not my pain

They are just roadblocks

That proves how far I came.

PRINCIPLE'S FROM RANDELL'S STORY

PRINCIPLE 1:

Acceptance

We cannot control the situations, events, circumstances nor people life throws our way. It is beyond us. We do however have control over our response to these things. Acceptance is looking at the situation with open eyes and accepting the situation as is. Understanding our true power lies in responding to every situation rather than reacting to them. Acceptance is a powerful yet undervalued mindset. When we accept the circumstances, situations, events and people that come in our lives we are liberated from the needless self-inflicted pain and suffering we experience. Accepting the situation at hand is vital because when we resist the present moment before us, we are essentially telling the universe that it's wrong. Accepting the situation is critically looking at the situation without judgement but with an open mind and heart. When I decided to accept what happened to me not as being a victim, but rather as someone given a second chance at life, I was automatically liberated. I chose to stay optimistic knowing that my wounds were not going anywhere but rather they would be a reminder of what could have happened. In our lives, we are all going to experience some form of hardship and adversity, but it has 90% to do with our frame of mind.

PRINCIPLE 2:

Responsibility

I know you've heard this word many times before. Broken down it is simply our ability to respond. In every situation, we can react to what happens or respond to what happens. Taking responsibility for our role in every situation can be tough but so vital to our growth. In every situation, that life throws our way we always have a choice. Although we cannot choose what happens to us or who decides to throw their poison our way, we always have a choice as to how we respond to the situations we face. Ultimately, if someone does something that upsets us, if we allow their poison to impact us, that is a choice, a reaction. We have to take responsibility for our own roles in every situation. I am not saying if someone hurts you, you shouldn't be hurt. What I am saying is that we have to realize we are always responsible for our part in every situation. Someone has hurt us and just because they are in a negative space, doesn't mean that we have to bring ourselves down to that level. I took responsibility for my role in what happened.

Obviously, I couldn't predict what was going to happen that night, but I put myself in a situation where this could have happened. The group of friends shooting guns in the air probably were not the best people to be around after a round of gunshots had caused chaos that night. I realized that I was responsible for my choice to go and meet with those guys and that at the very best I walked away with my life. Maybe if we had made it to those friends before the stabbing took place, the police could have stopped us and we all could have ended up in jail that night with a record for gun possession. Of course, I didn't know I was going to get mugged and stabbed but I had to step back and look at my choices and recognize I did some things that put me in a situation where this could happen.

PRINCIPLE 3:

Finding The Seeds Of Opportunity In Every Adversity

In every situation, there is a learning opportunity. It's all about our perspective though. We can choose to see a situation as harmful or "bad" based on our perspective. I believe it's important to note that "good" and "bad" are subjective based on our interpretation and beliefs. Good and bad are not real; perception determines what they are. In every adversity lies a seed of opportunity to learn and grow from, if we choose to see it that way. Life is never working against us but for us.

In these situations, it is asking yourself, what can I learn from this situation? How can this situation help me get closer to where I want to be? Why did this happen to me and how can I grow from this experience? This practice will take time to develop. Every time you approach an obstacle, take a mental step back and remember that how you respond is your choice. You can choose to judge yourself and be victim to the situation or you can choose to be an alchemist and ask the questions above.

I took away many seeds of opportunity. Obviously changing my friends and my environment was the first thing I had to do to avoid finding myself in these situations again. What I learned from this situation is that no matter what situations we do go through, we have to find the inner strength to fight and conquer these battles and not let these battles conquer us. I also realized that material things do not bring happiness into our lives. Rather they are tools that bring happiness to the surface. I really learned that happiness is found within an individual and that new designer shoes do not necessarily make me happy. The biggest seed of opportunity was that I now had a purpose in life. I had something to live for. If I didn't, I truly do believe the Most High would have called me up. I knew from that moment there was something inside of me that really needed to manifest. It was a hard way to learn but sometimes life has these amazing ways of teaching us valuable lessons through painful experiences. I do not regret what happened to me in the slightest bit. It gave me a story to share with others in hopes of inspiring. It also gave me the belief in myself, that if I put my mind to anything I do, I will accomplish it. Even if it means defying the odds and bouncing back from near death experiences.

RANDELL ADJEI

Randell Adjei is an entrepreneur, speaker and spoken word practitioner who uses his gifts to empower through Edutainment. He is the founder of one of Toronto's largest youth led initiatives: Reaching Intelligent Souls Everywhere (R.I.S.E Edutainment). In 2018, R.I.S.E received the Toronto Arts Foundation's, Mayor's Youth Arts Award. Randell is the author of "I am Not my struggles," a powerful Anthology released in 2018. Highly decorated, Randell was the 2015 Best Spoken Word recipient for the Black Canadian Awards and was also named 2015's Torontonian of the Year by one of Canada's national broadcast channels. Due to his continuous community and mentorship work, Randell was also recognized as a Local Hero in 2017 by the NOW Magazine,

Website: Randelladjei.com

Social Media: @randelladjei

CHAPTER SEVEN

GROWTH FROM ADVERSITY
BY JOSEPH ACQUAYE

"Good timber does not grow with ease. The stronger the wind,
the stronger the trees"

J. Willard Marriot

- I was in tenth grade, failing ninth grade French the second time and had been on the brink of expulsion for possession of marijuana with intent to distribute.
- I had just graduated university with high honours, but not accepted into any of the professional programs I applied to and found myself without a job and without a car (stolen out of my driveway).
- Accepted to medical school, no bank was willing to provide me with a loan due to my family financial situation; forcing me to consider declining my admission.
- I was in my third year of medical school, undecided as to what specialty I wanted to pursue and I would find out my eldest sister passed away from cancer.

The common thread in all these experiences is growth from adversity and that is what I hope to convey to you, the reader, as I delve into these experiences and more.

CHAPTER SEVEN

My name is Joseph Acquaye; I am 30 years old and currently live in Minneapolis, Minnesota. I currently work at the University of Minnesota as a third-year resident in the Department of Urology (this is a medical specialty focused on the surgical management of bladder, prostate, kidney, penile and testicular cancers and other diseases). I am married to my wife of almost 3 years who works as a registered nurse and we recently welcomed our first son. By many accounts, to borrow from my native Toronto-lingo, I'm blessed fam (fair warning, I will be deferring to my Toronto-lingo often and will provide explanations as needed; "fam" is short for family and refers to a person or group of people). However, as alluded to in my introduction, this story is not about my destination but about the journey and its numerous challenges. This story is about growth through adversity. This is my story.

I was born in Toronto, Ontario (more specifically in Rexdale) to two parents who had recently emigrated from Ghana to Toronto. Both my parents had not received anything greater than secondary education and had hustled and navigated their way through an intricate immigration system to make it here. I had three other siblings: one older half-sister and two younger sisters. We experienced the challenges faced by many immigrant families but my parents sought to make the most of their opportunity in this country. Given their limited education there were very few professional opportunities afforded to them however as I mentioned earlier, they had a hustler mentality. My mother, who was working as a personal care assistant at a nursing home at the time, noted that there were very few black owned beauty supply stores. She decided she wanted to change that and started selling hair care products out of our basement. The basement became a flea market, the flea market became a store within a mall and one store became multiple stores. She ran the business with my father who had worked as a truck driver and pharmacy tech prior.

Throughout elementary school I found myself in trouble pretty often. Illustrative of this point was the fact that I was in detention hall so often that when I was actually able to attend second recess it was a highly publicized event. Like many young boys my age, my priorities were video games, girls and sports with academic success being very low on that list. I competed on the track and field team and experienced great success in the high jump and short sprints. My purpose at that time was deeply tied to athletics and like many young athletes I had dreams of competing at the highest level. Unfortunately, my tendency to get in trouble would prevent me from competing in eighth grade. While I caused trouble for most of my teachers, no one bore the brunt of that greater than my French teacher. Case in point, on one occasion I was asked to recite a sentence in French that we were told to memorize. Instead, I proceeded to recite a line from "Lady Marmalade" a popular (and inappropriate) song at that time. The line was "Voulez vous coucher avec moi ce soir" (roughly translated to "Do you want to sleep with me tonight"). As usual, I had everyone laughing at my antics, but for her this was the last straw. I was brought to the office, reprimanded and kicked off the track and field team. I did not take this well and had a few words I won't repeat with her and my home room teacher. The damage was already done however and I missed the chance to compete in the regional championships in which I was a favorite to win. Missing the opportunity to compete meant missing an opportunity to be recruited by athletically inclined high schools and my aspirations of high level competition no longer seemed attainable.

I share the above-mentioned story to illustrate how our well thought out plans and goals can be derailed by our own actions. With a lack of recruitment opportunities, the initial high schools I had hoped to attend were no longer in reach and I instead sought to attend the high school all my friends were going to. My mom however put a hard stop to this knowing that I would only find myself getting into further trouble if I stayed with this crew throughout high school. Instead, I found out I would be attending St. Basil-The-Great College School. I would not know anyone and essentially find myself having to start fresh. As you can imagine "mans was marved" (in Toronto-lingo "mans" refers to yourself or a group of people and "marved" means annoyed). Moving from a place of familiarity and starting anew is something that people often go through and some are able to adapt to these changes easier than others. For me, this would be a big challenge and I tried to return to something that was familiar—track and field.

Though I was not attending a school known for their track and field success they did have a fairly good team. I quickly made friends with my new teammates and was set to compete in the regional championships. On the day of the track meet, I remember missing the team bus ride (due to the fact that I unfortunately operated on AST, "African Standard Time") and had to take the public bus to the meet. I arrived with a few minutes to spare and had to quickly prepare for my race. Normally my preparation was long consisting of stretching and drills, but I did not have the time and unwisely proceeded to my race without warming up.

I lined up at the start line, heard the gun fire, took my first few strides and then felt a pop followed by a burning pain in the back of my right leg. I did not finish the race that day; I had to be helped off the field by my dad who was watching in the stands. Diagnosis: severe quadriceps tendon tear. Recovery: six weeks. Track season: over (and possibly my track career). This was a turning point in my high school career and would send me down an unfortunate path. Returning to school after the injury saw me returning to square one. I wasn't able to hang out with the friends I had made during track and field and often spent lunches sitting alone. I was not very motivated in the classroom and had difficulty keeping up with the course work. My grades began to slide and I particularly struggled in French class. On the final exam, in an act of defiance (but more so stupidity), I remember drawing an unflattering sketch of my teacher on the exam paper and not answering a single question.

Needless to say I would be taking that class over again. I concluded my first year of high school with mostly C's and D's—not exactly a strong start.

The following year was where my troubles would catch up to me. I came into the school year with a new group of friends (some of which I had met over the previous summer break) and a new focus. Not on the classroom, but on the distribution of marijuana and illegal paraphernalia. Over the summer, I had learned a bit about this business and the opportunities to make more money than I could imagine as a 14-year-old kid with no allowance. Being the child of immigrant parents means the only allowance you have is being allowed to live in the house. My friends and the higher ups who supplied us with the product to distribute reassured me that as long as we did as instructed we would not find ourselves in trouble. The instructions were simple, bring said product to school, store it in a locker, check the locker at the end of the day and get paid. All the while I was barely attending classes and taking French again. On my second go at this class, I had hoped to avoid the same teacher by switching to the lower difficulty French class but to my surprise, he switched as well and to no one's surprise, we did not get along.

It was a normal day in French class and I was seated at the back of the class. If you have ever watched any movie about drug dealing, you know one of the cardinal rules is, "Don't get high on your own supply." I usually followed this rule however on this day I was feeling particularly bored and adventurous (a bad combination) and decided I was going to "tump" a backwoods after class (in Toronto slang this means smoke some weed rolled in a backwoods cigar, a popular brand of rolling paper). As I was rolling up the backwoods at the back of class, my French teacher noticed I was up to something and demanded to know what. I quickly pocketed the rolled backwoods and refused to let him inspect me further. He had it with me and brought me down to the principal's office where I would have no choice but to be searched. Sensing that the situation was becoming serious, I knew I had to somehow rid myself of the evidence. As I was being marched down to the office, I caught the eye of one of my friends and motioned to her to come over. In one quick moment, I was able to reach in my pocket and hand off the rolled backwoods to her. As I was brought before the principal, he demanded that I empty my pockets, which I gladly did and of course, there was nothing to show. At this moment, my French teacher was adamant that I had something in my pocket and began to cite numerous instances where I had acted out in class.

I had thought I had the last laugh but after all my misdeeds had been presented to the principal I was threatened with expulsion and a call was made to my parents. The most terrifying thing about this experience was not the threat of expulsion but the fact that they called my parents. Any child of immigrants knows there are few fates worse than facing your parents after they get a call from school. My mother was able to smooth the situation over with the principal and gave me an ultimatum. Smarten up or pack your bags and get on a plane to Ghana to attend boarding school. She was finally fed up with me after all I had put her through. As I look back, I'm sure that my parents did not have enough money to fly me anywhere but the threat alone was motivation enough to try and change. I immediately withdrew myself from any further dealings with drugs and escaped from the situation relatively unscathed however one of my good friends was not so lucky.

This friend was older, funny and athletic. He had all the traits I hoped to emulate, especially his way with the ladies. I met him over the summer working at the shop with my dad. One aspect about the drug business that I was acutely aware of was the fact that you will inevitably make enemies (even among those who were once friends) and sadly he would learn this the hard way. He was walking home one evening and it was just past midnight when he heard a few steps approaching in the quiet of the night. Immediately sensing something was not right, he ran in the opposite direction but it would be too little too late. Multiple shots were fired, one of which hit his spine. He would survive but was to spend the rest of his life in a wheel chair. This was an eye opening experience for me and a salient reminder of the fate that I could potentially meet if I continued to go in the direction I was going.

This would be one of two experiences in the 10th grade that would have a lasting effect on my life. The other was finding my faith. After the above experience, I returned to school emotionally distraught but with a new sense of purpose. I was determined to get through the rest of 10th grade even if it meant barely scraping by. I did not know what to do with the mix of emotions, but knew I had to keep moving forward. I passed all my classes including French (though I can now admit, I had a bit of "help" on the final exam... hey I didn't say I was perfect, but for the young readers I do not condone cheating) and ushered in the next summer break. That summer I spent an afternoon with a childhood friend whom attended the same church I did. I often went to church with my parents, but this was more out of obligation than desire. Try telling an African mom you don't want to attend church and see how that goes. This friend was different from what I remembered and what struck me was his newfound passion regarding his Christian faith. I found this somewhat strange but I was intrigued and inquired further.

He revealed to me that he had attended a weekend church event called "The Encounter" and explained it as an opportunity to immerse yourself in your faith and get close to God. I was not interested and brushed this opportunity aside. That is until this girl, who happened to be a friend of my sister, suggested I go. This girl was tall, dark and beautiful with curves in all the right places. She had almond-shaped eyes, model-like cheekbones and thick lips. Her name was Precious and she certainly lived up to that title. I knew there was something special about her and little did I know, one day she would become my wife. After her suggestion, I was suddenly more inclined to attend (I would later tell her that I thought this would be an opportunity to score some points with her and maybe get some action). I decided to attend this encounter and much to my disappointment she was not there, I felt like I had been tricked and was determined to just get through the weekend and go home.

This would not be the case and I would not leave that weekend the same. Of the numerous lessons that we received from the numerous preachers and speakers at the event, the following would standout to me, "See yourself as God sees you." This simple revelation was life changing. Like many young people, I struggled with my identity and sense of importance. I wanted to fit in. I wanted to be accepted and the ways in which I sought to do so had led me down the wrong path. With this revelation however, I realized that my self-worth was not tied to what others thought about me but what God thought about me. Psalms 139:13-14 states, "You formed my inward parts; you covered me in my mother's womb. I will praise you, for I am fearfully and wonderfully made." I recognized this and would go forward with this mindset.

Returning to school that year, I had a much different focus and sense of purpose. I knew the potential I had in Christ and was determined to realize this potential. I kept all my classes in the university stream despite the fact my guidance counsellor adamantly suggested that I pursue a college route or a route leading to trade school. In time, my grades started to reflect my renewed effort and I would finish with the highest grade in my biology class. Another pivotal experience during this time was my acceptance to participate in the University of Toronto Summer Mentorship Program. This program began as an initiative to promote the health sciences to Black and Aboriginal students, both traditionally underrepresented in the health care fields. The importance of this was that it was my first time exposed to a different narrative of the Black high school student. These were students who sought to pursue post-secondary education and had a passion for learning. We came from the same places, experienced the same discrimination and overcame the same challenges. Additionally, this was the first time I would meet health professionals who looked like me. One individual in particular, Dr. Joel Kerr a Chiropractor, had an especially important influence on me.

I saw myself in him, I saw the potential I had for success in him and most importantly I saw a future greater than I had ever envisioned for myself in him.

I had a new goal, and that was to pursue a career in the medical field. Returning to school the following year I would experience further academic and athletic success. I became a top performer in class and a top performer on the track. This would culminate in being the first student in school history to be awarded athlete of the year, top all-around male and valedictorian. I was then accepted to the University of Toronto to pursue a degree in physical education and health. I was awarded numerous scholarships and earned a spot on the varsity track and field team. By the time I started university, I felt as though I was ready to conquer the world. One recurring theme you will soon notice however is that things would not be as easy as I had hoped.

Midway through my first year things were not looking good. I was failing chemistry, barely passing my other courses and my performance on the track was far below my expectations. In addition, my parents' business was not doing well and things became much more difficult financially. The new financial difficulties placed a significant strain on my parents' relationship. One evening on the way back from school on a particularly long day I came home to the sight of packed luggage in the living room. When I inquired what was happening, my dad told me he was moving out and was unsure about how long he would be gone. My dad and I had an up and down relationship, but I considered him a great source of support and inspiration. Additionally, the emotions my mom felt regarding this separation were often directed at me. By the end of my first year I had a marginal GPA, a strained relationship with both my parents and ended up quitting the track and field team in order to work.

I had all but lost hope in my dream of pursuing a medical profession and was unsure if I would be able to complete my degree. I was however fortunate enough to have a great support system of friends whom I had met during my first year. They were people who remained positive in the midst of adversity and encouraged me to do the same. They never let me get down on myself and when I did, they would not let me remain there. I relied on my friends, I relied on my faith, I relied on my mentors and I relied on the lessons I had learned from my failures. Doing so carried me through the next few years of my undergraduate studies. By the time I had reached my final year I had received numerous scholarships and awards and had improved my GPA significantly. I made the decision to apply for medical school and in order to do so I had to take the Medical Colleges Admissions Test (MCAT). The first time I sat for this exam was in my third year. I was convinced this exam was going to be a breeze but soon realized that wasn't the case after getting my results and landing below the 10th percentile for performance. Nonetheless, when I graduated I would be one of the few students in my program awarded high honours and applied to medical school, believing that my academic performance would outweigh my performance on the MCAT. I recognized however that this was a longshot and applied to other master's programs as a backup plan.

The application responses started to roll in and the header was always the same, "We regret to inform you." After ten rejections and zero acceptances, I found myself in an interesting situation. I was a newly minted graduate with no plan for post-graduate education and student loans knocking on my door. To add insult to injury, the same morning I received my final rejection was the same morning I woke up to my car missing from my driveway. Mans was cheesed (in Toronto-lingo "cheesed" means annoyed). While I was discouraged, I thought that I would be able to find some type of work as a new graduate. Again, I applied to numerous positions and after many weeks of searching, received only a single response. The University of Toronto parking services were looking for new custodial staff. I accepted. My job would entail cleaning up garbage around campus. This was the same campus where I had spent the last 4 years and as such I knew many students and staff who still frequented the campus. I would run into these people in my work clothes cleaning up their trash. This was certainly a humbling experience and would serve as my main income for the next 2 years.

As I worked this job, I normally wore a particular shirt I had received at a conference years prior, which stated, "Knowledge is power." I often received offhand comments whenever I wore this shirt as people thought it ironic that I would wear this shirt while cleaning up trash at a university campus. The reason I continued to wear this shirt is because I knew that the words rang true and I knew that through this job I would save up enough money to take additional courses, improve my GPA, retake the MCAT exam and re-apply to medical school. I did just that and after applying to over 30 medical schools I would receive a single interview at Meharry Medical College in Nashville, Tennessee. I remember the 24-hour trip because I could not afford a flight directly from Toronto. I remember getting housed by someone I knew through a friend of a friend who graciously hosted me and let me practice interviewing with him. I remember travelling back to Toronto convinced I had done horrible on my interview. Most importantly, I remember the morning of December 19, 2011 opening an email, which had an unfamiliar subject line, "Congratulations, you have been admitted to the first year class at Meharry Medical College."

"I did it! I finally did it I'm going to medical school," was my first thought however, this acceptance would introduce yet another obstacle. Medical school in the US is not cheap and getting a loan would prove not only to be a challenge, but next to impossible. Both my parents did not have adequate credit and I had used all my savings for this application process. I went to every major bank, I petitioned to former professors and supervisors, I asked for help from whomever I could think of but everything was to no avail. Six months later, I was en route to yet another bank (I had lost count by this time) and I received an e-mail from Meharry saying that my admission would be rescinded if I could not demonstrate proof of funds within the next 3 weeks. After all this work, I was about to have this accomplishment stripped away from me. I felt I had exhausted all my options and was ready to give up my admission and my dream of attending medical school. Shortly after receiving that e-mail however, I received a call from an uncle who had heard about the situation from my mom. He attended church with a banker who suggested that if I could find another family member to co-sign my loan for me I would be able to secure it in time.

Asking someone who wasn't my immediate family to co-sign such a hefty loan for me was not something that had crossed my mind, but by this point I had no choice. I explained the situation to another uncle whom had helped to care for me when I was younger and without hesitation, he offered to co-sign. The only stipulation is that he would need to put his house down as an asset to help secure this loan which he did. The status of my loan was still in doubt however, I decided to organize a going away party prior to receiving confirmation. People who were aware of the situation thought I was crazy for organizing a party before actually securing the funds. I had faith that everything would work out. The same morning I made the down payment for the party venue, I received a phone call. My loan had been approved.

Medical school would serve as one of the more rewarding and engaging academic experiences of my life and despite early struggles it was enjoyable. I also enjoyed the unique opportunity to attend a historically black medical school with classmates, professors and physicians who all looked like me. I also discovered another passion of mine in tutoring classmates. At times, the evening tutorial sessions I held would be larger than the actual classes. I continue to see the fruits of my labour as former students of mine graduate and enter the work force as dentists and physicians. During my third year of medical school, I received a call from my younger sister informing me that my older sister was admitted to the hospital with what was thought to be a respiratory infection. I did not think much of it at the time and was certain she would recover. She was a young, healthy and vibrant lady who taught exercise classes in her spare time. I would later learn that this was not merely a simple infection.

By the latter half of my third year, I had decided that I wanted to pursue a surgical specialty. I was in the middle of my surgery rotation and enjoying my experience with urology so much that I thought about selecting this specialty. I was initially discouraged from doing so given the competitive nature of this specialty. This specialty typically attracts the top medical students based on exam scores and research experience. Of the thousands of competitive applicants who apply, only approximately 420 will receive interviews and of this, approximately 290 will be hired to train at one of the 70 plus training centres across the country who will each take one to five trainees a year. With this knowledge I was very hesitant to begin preparing my application and continued to put it off. Then one night I received the bad news. My sister did not have a respiratory infection, she had leukemia and her prognosis was very poor. A month later, I would be informed that she had passed away at the age of 32.

My sister Cecilia served as one of my main sources of inspiration and losing her so suddenly was a very emotional experience. As I reflected on her life, I remembered that she constantly imparted on me the following two lessons. The first was the importance of looking at every experience, both good and bad, in a positive light. The second was going after every opportunity regardless of other people's reservations. Her untimely passing was a reminder that life is not guaranteed and while her life was cut short, she lived a full one. I was determined to do the same. After returning to school, I put my residency application together and applied to urology.

The application process was quite daunting and I can only thank my soon-to-be wife Precious at the time for working overtime and taking out bank loans in order to help finance the numerous flights, application costs, hotel stays, bus rides and car rentals. I found myself travelling to multiple states in the span of a few days and when I could not afford a hotel or other accommodation, I would take my luggage and sleep wherever I could including an iHop and a bus terminal. After 15 interviews spanning 11 states and 30 flights, I had finally completed my interview trail. I felt confident about my odds for securing a training spot. Not because I was more qualified than other applicants (I was often the only student who didn't attend an Ivy League school, have family members who were physicians or have numerous publications to my name) but because my story of how I had gotten to this point stood out. A few weeks later, I would find out that I was one of the 50 applicants interviewed to receive a training spot at the University of Minnesota. I graduated medical school with highest honours and relocated to Minnesota to begin residency.

As a third-year resident, I am currently a little more than halfway through this latest chapter of my life. It has been fraught with daily challenges and is mentally and physically demanding but also very rewarding. As I reflect on the story I shared I think about the lessons I've learned along the way. It is these same lessons that give me the strength to face these daily challenges with confidence and poise. My challenges, trials, tribulations and triumphs are not yours but I hope that the lessons embedded in the story are some that you take to heart. Be persistent, recognize your worth, find mentors, surround yourself with positive people and do not let failures define you. We are 10 men, we have one mission and that is to inspire you the reader to realize your potential and author your own success story.

PRINCIPLES FROM JOSEPH'S STORY

PRINCIPLE 1:

It's Not About How You Start, It's How You Finish

When pursuing a goal, stay focused regardless of the challenges you may initially encounter. It is this focus which will help you ultimately reach your goal.

PRINCIPLE 2:

Your Perception Of Self Will Determine Your Attitude

We are often concerned with what other people think, and that can determine how we think and act. The most important opinion however is your opinion of yourself, because that will determine how you work towards your goals.

PRINCIPLE 3:

Surround Yourself With People Who Will Lift You Up

As you work towards your goals, you will encounter many people. Not everyone you encounter is ready to help you work towards your goals. Be around people who will continually motivate and encourage you even when you are down on yourself, these people will be the same to celebrate with you once you reach your goal.

PRINCIPLE 4:

Be Positive

This is a simple principle but often easier said than done. A positive mindset is what will give you the endurance to keep working towards your goals despite seemingly insurmountable obstacles.

PRINCIPLE 5:

See Each Obstacle As A Stepping-Stone

We often see the obstacles we face in a negative light, but each obstacle is a stepping-stone and a lesson. The purpose of these lessons is to equip you with the skills, connections and experiences needed to excel once you've reached your goal.

JOSEPH ACQUAYE

Joseph Acquaye is a Ghanaian-Canadian born and raised in Rexdale, ON. He attended St. Basil-the-Great College school and after some initial difficulties he graduated as Athlete of the Year, Top All-round male and Valedictorian. He then attended the University of Toronto where he graduated with a degree in Physical Education and Health and participated on the Varsity Track and Field team. He continued his post-graduate studies at York University. He then attended medical school at Meharry Medical College where he graduated as president of the Medical School Honor Society. He is currently completing his residency in urology at the University of Minnesota Medical Center. He currently lives in Minneapolis with his wife and son.

Social Media: @jakademik_md

CHAPTER EIGHT

DECIDING MY WAY THROUGH

BY KEITH HILL JR.

Growing up there were many uncertainties in my young life – even though I wasn't aware of them at the time. I wasn't aware because my single-mother of five "active" children was constantly making decisions to provide for our needs. As I got older and journeyed through life's difficulties, the uncertainties of being self-employed and of life overall, I had to make decisions of my own. Looking back, I realize that negative outcomes occurred when I made decisions mostly out of feelings and without enough thought. The man I am today now makes better decisions and the result has been positive.

Currently, I am a part-time professor and a business owner. Working in both capacities and through living life overall, decisions must be made on a regular basis. What I've learned and the question I pose is, "What's the best way to react when faced with a decision?" My story deals with how I "decided my way" through three difficult situations: the loss of loved ones, marriage and self-control.

Throughout life, especially when in a difficult position, decisions must be made, ranging from those made in the immediate sense to ones that require lengthy deliberation. When we decide, we do so by using feelings (heart-led) and/or by careful deliberation (thought-led). As we all face decisions, I ask, what is the best guide to bring you out or keep you out of a problem? What's your decision-making process? When you're in that deciding moment, how do you react?

Life is 10% what happens to you and 90% how you react to it.

Charles R. Swindoll

The Loss of Loved Ones

Several years ago, I lost my sister to leukemia. The following year my aunt died from heart failure. Three years later, one of my closest friends passed away from cancer. Despite the difficulty of each situation, I had to find a way to continue living life with some sense of normalcy. Initially, I couldn't imagine how I could pick up the pieces from this kind of blow to the heart, but I had to learn.

The day after my sister's passing; I was naturally overcome with grief. Family and friends flooded the house with their condolences. However, I was not in the mood – I stayed locked away in the bedroom for three days. During this time, I wrestled with God. "How could a God-fearing woman not get the blessing of healing?" It was during this time that I came to the revelation: it's OK to be angry but it's not OK to let the anger be my guide. It's OK to be hurt, but just like any other pain, find a way to heal.

Once I came to these realizations, I had to find a way to get out of bed. I began thinking to myself, "Is staying locked away from everybody conducive to my healing – or to anything? According to my faith, is she not in a better place?" I asked myself these questions and a host of others. Also, being self-employed I had to come to the reality that I didn't have the luxury of bereavement or sick days. In the end, I knew that I had to find a way out before I sunk in deeper. By the fourth day, I was able to get out of the bed.

Once I ultimately internalized the thought that I had no choice – or rather, that the alternative was detrimental to my mental and financial health, I knew I had to act. Before I get into what I did, let me discuss another situation.

Marriage

I was married for 14 years. However, we spent most of that time physically and/or emotionally separated. She is a good woman and we did try; the church, counseling, you name it, but I sometimes wonder why we didn't end our relationship long before we did. Better yet, should we have even moved forward in the first place? I've looked back, considered these questions and learned many things about marriage and myself in the process.

It is said that the only thing we look for with great effort more than money is love. Yet we often strategize about the former and not the latter. I know in my case, the love I had in my marriage was never coupled with the serious questions necessary to quantify our compatibility, goals, shortcomings and strengths. In other words, more thought should've been put in. If while dating, there are things of concern that become uncovered through conversation or observation then you need to ask yourself, "If this situation never changes, can I spend my life with this person?" If the answer is yes, then you are blessed. If the answer is no, then you got some more thinking to do! For me, I learned this lesson the hard way.

I remember being at an extreme low point in my marriage and speaking to a couple of friends who were also at low points in their marriages. After hearing them vent, it made me go back to my relationship with the warped perspective that it was the norm to have drama in marriages. That anger and frustration just came with the territory, but marriage doesn't have to be a nightmare. The older wiser me knows this. My current relationship and witnessing many others over the years, is my evidence. Many people live in unhealthy relationships, trapped by their emotions. Whether that emotion is love, fear or complacency. We need to take the time to "think" about the relationships we find ourselves in and then act accordingly to avoid or get free from the trap. Thoughts like, what do I need from my partner? What can I do differently that would benefit the relationship? Is it sensible that we stay together?

Thinking then acting means being happier in relationships. Alternatively, it could mean realizing that you are better off getting out. Now I'm not encouraging divorce, because on the other hand, we often exit serious relationships without giving enough thought to what can help make the situation better. The relationship just ends because someone doesn't "feel" the love anymore without trying to figure out what went wrong and how to get it back on track.

Operating on feelings alone gives you only half of the perspective. Relationships are work and work requires thought, calculation and decision-making. Often, we just use love as the guide (insert violins here). Mature relationships need more than that one leg to stand on. If you don't have another one, two, three or more legs, then when you don't feel the love, what do you have to lean on in those moments until the love returns? It's like the advice about loving both the interior and the exterior of your partner. If based on something superficial like youthful beauty, then what will keep you attracted when that beauty fades?

Many times, we enter serious relationships feeling that love is enough to make the relationship work. Love is necessary, obviously, but "love" is both a noun and a verb. The noun is where the emotion lives, you are "in love" but the verb is "to love" and that's where the action or "thought" comes from.

Before going any further here, let's look at one more example of a heart-led decision vs. a thought-led one.

Is it Worth It?

I used to be the king of road rage; OK maybe it wasn't that bad, but it was bad. Most people who know me as calm, cool, collected Keith probably can't imagine this, but it's true (I blame it on too many years of living in Brooklyn). Cutting off another driver for cutting me off first; speeding down the highway after them if they decided to make a break for it. In addition, there are the few occasions when I ended up getting out of the car. Wow.... even as I write this it sounds crazy.

How can I develop such anger towards a stranger?! Going from, travelling to my destination in peace, to ending up in dangerous scenarios while driving – getting so mad that the senseless anger dictates how I drive. All in the name of retaliation or revenge – not to a sworn enemy, but to a total stranger! All of this because emotions got the best of me.

I remember years later, as the mature version of myself, I was driving and someone sped past me, giving me the finger. I was confused. He then cut right in front of me in what I could tell was in revenge to something I did or to something he thought I did. After he swerved in front of me, he slammed on his brake, then sped off – heated! I kept my cool, almost feeling sorry for him.

Then we got to a traffic light and we were beside each other. I lowered the car window and offered an apology as a good gesture. He wasn't trying to hear it.

With a fully frowned face, he sat there fuming, then as soon as the light changed to green, he flipped the bird again and sped off like the green light signaled the start of a race. I casually drove off at my own pace thinking to myself, "Wow, I never want to be that guy again – that sucks." If they thought about the whole ordeal, they would likely agree (if they were in their right mind) how ridiculous and unnecessary it was to react that way and that it's better to just peacefully go on about their day – that's if they thought about it.

"You will continue to suffer if you have an emotional reaction to everything that is said to you. True power is sitting back and observing everything with logic; true power is restraint. If words control you that means everyone else can control you; breathe and allow things to pass."

Anonymous

The Head or the Heart
So, what am I trying to say?

The common denominator in each story above and in so many other situations is that we often just react. No thought, all feeling.

Whether the feeling is in response to a heartbreaking event (like the death of someone close to you), or a deep emotional gut feeling to something life changing (like marriage), or maybe it's just a kneejerk reaction to something trivial (like road rage). Whatever is being decided, whatever the situation, all I'm saying is that at worst, make it a two-part process; check in with your emotion but confirm with your logic.

Gaining After a Loss

After losing my sister I had to acknowledge that staying wrapped up in bed wasn't going to help me move on, even though I "felt" like it – as a matter of fact, I knew if I didn't get out of the bed, it would have made things worse. I had to "think" about what I needed instead. First and foremost, I leaned in heavy on my faith. With each loss, I thought to myself, yes, I missed them, but they are in a better place and when my time comes, I will see them again. Also, I ended up surrounding myself with people and things that helped. I was selective about who and what I was around; one of those things was comedy. I enjoy a good laugh and I tried to sit in front of as much comedy shows and movies that I could find; there's nothing like a good chuckle to shake off some of the blues. Another thing was work. Considering that my work takes a lot of concentration, ironically, I found that getting lost in my work was helpful.

These were strategies used to prevent me from falling into a deep hole of depression, stress or even a loss of faith. If I followed my feelings down the road they wanted to take me, I would "be no good" right now, to this day – at all. Your needs may be different than mine, but ultimately, whatever works for you is what you must do. My point is, you must understand what that is and in order to understand it, you must think about it. This mindset doesn't only apply to the most extreme situations.

When faced with difficulties, whether it's an everyday challenge or a life altering tragedy, by default, we are led by our feelings.

These feelings dictate how we act and our actions can end up perpetuating the feelings. Typically, this cycle slants towards a negative outcome. The result, a downward spiral into a place no one wants to go but a place where many end up. In these instances, your entire being just wants to react on how you "feel", especially when the feelings are strong. However, in these difficult times – correction: ESPECIALLY, in these difficult times, feelings must never be the deciding factor; your best actions are made when "thought" is also put to it.

Let me stop here for a moment and say, I'm not suggesting this will be easy. I'm not saying it was easy for me. Matter of fact, going against your natural inclination of following your emotions to wherever they may lead you is hard! Yes, hard, but the benefit makes it worth it.

Trust me; the prison system is filled with those who wish they could go back to the incident, which led them to incarceration and re-think about it before acting.

Relating in Relationships

In marriage or even before the engagement, beyond the love you have for each other, there should be things that are considered and thought about to qualify compatibility. Such as, is the thing you dislike the most about your partner a deal breaker should it never change? For men, is she willing to take your last name if that's something important to you? What are your financial goals and positions? What's your position on having children or blending families? Are there any cultural differences that are uniquely important? My ex-wife is American and my background is Jamaican; I didn't think about how I would miss the food of my culture!

Speaking of food, you must understand who can cook? Who will cook? Who wants to cook? Who's willing to learn to cook? Unless you are well off or heavily supported by a loving family/support system then this small consideration can become a big problem. This is vastly underestimated, especially when there are small children in the mix. This was a HUGE point of contention in my previous marriage and something I highly underestimated.

In my current relationship, I take nothing for granted. I take the lessons I learned with me as she and I continue to move forward. We've talked about many things when it comes to our needs, wants, shortcomings and strengths.

The point is, you must know who you're dealing with, so you can deal with them accordingly or know if you're prepared for what you must deal with and vice versa. Yes, you love the person. However, you need to know who you are. You need to know who they are. You need to know if those people even get along outside the confines of love and affection. I always say you must "like" the person you're with as much as you "love" them...or even more! Have you ever thought about that?!

Control Your Direction

Always back up emotion with reason. Emotional feeling can be anything from, "it just feels right" to being so angry that you literally and figuratively lose control of yourself. Oftentimes a quick second thought like, "Is this worth it?" could be all that you need to save you from so much grief.

Recently, coming from church a driver that was clearly in the wrong blatantly cut me off. I decided I wasn't letting him in. (Imagine the kind of struggle it takes if this can even happen after coming from church!) As our driving got more and more aggressive and we were inches from each other at times, my girl, who was in the passenger seat using her phone looked up and noticed what was going on, "What are you doing??" she said. I looked at her then immediately thought the exact same thing, "Yeah, what am I doing?" I simply changed lanes. In that split second, with one simple thought, I was able to avoid the potential danger of my surging emotions.

As a God-fearing man, I would be remiss if I didn't consider the ultimate deciding factor, which is God's Word.

My favorite scripture **2 Timothy 1:7 reads**:

For God did not give us a spirit of timidity or cowardice or fear, but [He has given us a spirit] of power and of love and of sound judgment and personal discipline [abilities that result in a calm, well-balanced mind and self-control].

When I unpack this passage, it's clear to me that God's aim for man is to go through their life and specifically through their challenges being led by their mind, not just their feelings.

Conversely **Proverbs 3:5 states:**

Trust in the Lord with all your heart and lean not on your own understanding

Now, if you are guided spiritually, then that trumps all. But, also remember that **James 2:17 says:**

So too, faith, if it does not have works [to back it up], is by itself dead...

Even faith, by itself is not enough; it must be followed by action. In the same manner, emotion is not enough; it must be followed by thought.

There's also a quote that encapsulates the gist of my message:

Move with strategy and not emotion.

My version of this quote is:

Move with thought and not just emotion.

Now I'm not suggesting you become disconnected from your feelings. Nor am I suggesting you become so "in your head" that you are robot-like and overly analytical. What I am suggesting is that if you react to ANY situation, good or bad, ENTIRELY out of emotion then you are gambling with the outcome. Conversely, when you put your mind to what you are going through, you increase the odds TREMENDOUSLY that the result will be in your favour. I had to learn this. Matter of fact, I still battle with it, but I now catch myself and don't let it get the best of me.

Some people argue that you should always "follow your gut" – usually referring to when you're at a fork in the road. If you're one of those "gut" people, all I'm saying is, it's OK to follow it BUT only after your mind does the final check and gives the OK to proceed.

There are many other examples I could have used to illustrate my point; where following either a negative emotion, like real anger, or even a positive one, like perceived serendipity brought about an undesirable outcome.

If I was trapped by emotions and couldn't tap into my decision-making ability, I wouldn't be able to decide my way through negative situations and into positive ones like I have. I decided to celebrate the life of loved ones that I've lost more so than mourn their death. I decided my way into a healthy and happy relationship with someone I'm compatible with. My driving tolerance is... well ... getting better (hey, I never said I was perfect)

This philosophy worked well for my mother and it continues to work well for me too. I hope this message resonates with you.

In summary, as the adage goes, "You must think before you act." As simple as that age-old wisdom is, we don't practice it enough; we tend to be more emotionally driven, especially in the most critical times. Imagine what your life would be like if your decision-making process was: feel it, think about it, then act on it – now, that's something to think about.

PRINCIPLES FROM KEITH'S STORY

PRINCIPLE 1:

Follow Your Heart But Always Take Your Mind With You

As difficult as your obstacles might be, it's important that you think first before reacting. Your emotions are important, but so are the thoughts that you think. Use both your head and your heart when making decisions.

PRINCIPLE 2:

To Think Before You Act

Take a second, take a minute, take a day – take whatever you need to think before you act or react. This is not only about major life decisions; always practice thought-led decision making in all areas.

PRINCIPLE 3:

It's Difficult But It's Possible

If you haven't figured it out by now, life can be downright difficult at times. Always know that it's possible to get through difficulties and to do things that are challenging. In this challenge, the only obstacles you face are self-imposed, so you are the only problem that stands in your own way.

PRINCIPLE 4:

It's What You Need To Help You Lead

At several junctures throughout every man's (or woman's) life, he is called to be a leader. He might lead himself through internal battles. He may become a leader of his peer group or perhaps he's the leader of his family. Maybe he's a leader of a business. Whatever the countless ways leadership can arise, leadership is from the vantage point of the head and not the heart. Where do you think that saying came from, "it's not personal, it's just business."

KEITH HILL JR.

Keith Hill Jr. was born in Toronto, Canada and has a varied background and skill set. As a writer, in 2016, Keith wrote and self-published "Fighting Fear & Doing Discipline" - a book about discipline and courage being keys to success. This led to keynote speaking engagements at several high schools and universities. He uses his eclectic background and the lessons he unpacks in his book, as the backdrop for his speaking engagements. Always one to evolve and push boundaries, Keith wrote and produced a TV pilot called "Ray & Nephew" released independently in 2019. As a legal professional, Keith recently served as the Legal Accounting Professor at George Brown College. Currently, Keith manages his own legal accounting company, "Bookkeeping Matters".

Social Media: @Keithhill.jr

CHAPTER NINE

MY LABEL DOES NOT DEFINE ME

BY NICHOLAS BARHAM

I honestly can't believe that I am here telling this story. It is difficult to share because even as I write this I have fears and shame about the stigmas that come with it. Well here we go.

My earliest memories of school are riddled with variations of me getting in trouble. I can remember the smell of the secretary's coffee and the cold feel of the cracked faux leather benches as they were basically my home away from home. I spent primary school days attempting to explain why I had punched, pinched and poked my peers or why I was unable to sit still through the story on the Magic Carpet. Something inside me was always bubbling; I often had to express it by blurting it out or whispering it to my best friend. Sometimes while I was working, a beat would come to me and I would tap it out in wild rhythms of percussion, channeling my inner drummer. Turning my desk into a Djembe drum was not popular in spaces that were reserved for quiet learners. I did not fit in. I had Attention Deficit Hyperactive Disorder better known as ADHD.

In my early years, my behaviour could have been chalked up to somewhat normal "boy" behaviour. I yearned to run and play. I was a student who would wait for recess break where I could be a star. One of the only places that I found solace throughout my early education was in the athletic field. At recess I could express myself; I was accepted as one of the elite out there. People would look up to me; choose me to be their partner or to join their team. When I was given the opportunity to see myself as champion, I would outwork everyone. This is where I would give my 100%, where my focus was never an issue. I could meet any challenge out on the concrete or field, never fearing failure, never lacking confidence.

My mother had me enrolled in soccer at a young age to help me burn some of the excess energy. This did not help curb my inattention in the classroom. The classroom was the opposite of my experience at recess. I definitely was not elite in the classroom. I had poor attention, my mind would be racing from one topic to the next, leapfrogging from the lesson to what was I going to eat for lunch or the last episode of The Fresh Prince of Bel Air. I would be stuck in this wormhole of thinking, mind whirling at Category 5, miles from the lesson where I started and never returning to the lesson until it was too late. My teachers would often notice I was away in the clouds and asked me to answer questions, knowing I had no clue because I was not listening. I would feel a lump in my throat and my stomach would drop as if I was heading down a roller coaster, all knowing that once again the teacher put me on display as the dumbest kid in class. These occurrences got so bad that one time I was getting a tutorial by a school dentist on oral hygiene and because I was not paying attention to her questions, she sent a note home to my mother requesting I get my hearing checked. I was last to be picked for every academic task because nobody wanted to work with the kid who couldn't do the work. This daily routine definitely had an eroding effect on how I viewed myself and I was slowly seeing the motivation to learn or be a part of my own education process falling apart. After completing elementary school, I transferred from public school to a private school when a relationship with my teacher had fallen apart. I didn't last at that private school two weeks before I was shipped back to my previous school where things had broken down. The thought of going to school often brought on feelings of anxiety that would further hinder my focus on learning.

In junior high school things did not improve for me, things may have gotten worse. Without the outlet of having recess, my anxiety, impulsivity and disengagement expanded. My grades really suffered in junior high. I would often hide my report card for months, if I could get away with it, because report cards came out near my birthday. Hiding it could help me get something I liked. It hurt to see my friends getting Super Nintendo or a new Chicago Bulls Jacket while I got some silk shirts or dress pants because my grades didn't meet my mother's expectations. I knew it was hard for my mother, who was doing it on her own and was the head of her class while in school. I knew that my performance in school didn't warrant me getting more free time to play leisurely, especially since I never did homework. My anxiety had risen during seventh grade; I often had bouts of extreme stomach pain and would sometimes throw up in thought of going to class. On a weekly basis, I would go home due to stomach pain because it was too much to bear. On some weeks, I would only be at school for three days. These gaps in my education definitely contributed to the hole I was already in. With my grades dwindling and everyone noticing, I had to develop thick skin. I was big for my age but not as big as some of the eighth graders in my school, so I had to toughen up to withstand the barrage of torment coming my way. I was not a kid that wanted to be taken lightly and would take most opportunities to prove it. I remember one incident in particular. I had brought my new basketball to school and was shooting around on the court during lunch. I missed the shot and an eighth grade student got the rebound. I asked him to pass the ball back. He refused and decided to take my ball and shoot around with it. I jumped straight into action running over and grabbed him by the collar, yelling at him to give my ball back or else. I of course had to visit the office with consequences following those actions.

Another altercation landed me in trouble at school when I got into another chest-puffing match with yet another grade eight student. One particular day I was at school during lunch break, I was hanging out at the basketball court. I sized up a student whom I thought was my match and decided to test his resolve. When he walked by me I purposely put out my foot and tripped him. He was a popular kid, with many friends who unbeknownst to me would defend him at all costs. As he fell to the ground, two or three students attempted to corral me but I was able to sidestep and flee for what seemed to be my life. They caught me that day and the grade eight students took turns holding me and trying out the latest WWE wrestling moves on me. My lack of self-regulation and impulsive behaviour was becoming problematic with real consequences.

My mother continued her search for answers because of my bad grades, poor social skills and my horrible relationship with my teachers. I was once again on the move to another school. My mother had heard of a private school that might be able to accommodate me, so part way through grade eight I went to a Seventh Day Adventist private school called Crawford Academy. I begged my mother to reconsider and send me back to my normal school so I could be with my friends but to no avail. At the new school I was once again a small fish, the school went from elementary all the way up to high school. Everyone knew each other and I was the odd man out. My approach at this new school was to be much more humble, I didn't know anyone at all. I had to adjust my approach and really work on my impulsivity and my social interaction. This was an opportunity to create a new narrative for myself, but old habits die hard. My organizational skills and work ethic were still very poor.

Unlike at my previous school, the teacher Mrs. Burgin-Hall at this new school was unwilling to accept my lack of interest in school and often challenged me. She was not willing to watch me fail and saw some potential in me. When I didn't do my homework, she made it clear that my work would be handed in and would make me stay after school to finish it. She worked on keeping me organized and really took interest in me being successful. Although she was really tough and I was frankly afraid of her, I appreciated her. Throughout the remainder of my grade eight year, I received the best grades in school up until that point. Although I was somewhat proud of my work, I continued to hide those report cards because I still didn't have confidence in my smarts and still considered myself dumb. I would sometimes secretly pull the report cards from between my mattress and look at them. A pinch of pride pierced my feelings of disappointment making me think that maybe I am not dumb.

After a summer of protest, my mother allowed me to return to school in my home neighbourhood. The costs of tuition and travel expenses had become too high for my single mother to bear so I was heading back to public school. At the time, I was ecstatic to be back with some friends close to home and no uniform or long travel to school. It was obvious that I had not matured enough at the private school because I returned right back to the same bad habits that Ms. Burgin-Hall had helped work out. My backpack and locker resembled a disaster area and probably should have been sectioned off. I showed up to class without my materials and seldom did my assignments or homework. I quickly found out that in high school teachers did not have the patience to work with a student who had impulsivity, inattention and organizational issues.

During my ninth grade year, I was in for a wakeup call. I remember being called down to the guidance office. I was failing again. This time the stakes were high, this time I was going to have to repeat part of the ninth grade and possibly switch schools to a business and technical institute. The Business and Technical Institute (B.T.I.) sounds like a very professional name, sounds like a place that has specialized skills and would teach students about working with their hands and about trades. I would imagine maybe at some point these schools were helping students, but the perception that I had during my high school experience was that this was just a dumping ground. An island for educational misfits. I would often hear horror stories of kids getting beat up, tied to trees, jumped and robbed. It sounded more like a prison setting than a school, where survival was paramount and there was no room for real educational growth. Although I had my share of fights, I was not prepared to attend and survive in this type of environment. I really did some deep reflection between the tears I shed at the thought of being classified as a BTI kid. That's what they called students who went to business and technical institute schools. I remember the feeling of hopelessness washing over me unsure of what was going to happen but sure that I was a disappointment once again.

My mother along with the support of my aunts fought to keep me at my school but my mother decided to get a psychological evaluation done on me to find out if something else was in play. During this process, I answered various questions surrounding my school performance and worked on some problem solving puzzles. Going into my tenth grade, I was diagnosed with ADHD with an emphasis on inattentiveness. For some kids that diagnosis is a bright flashing red sign that reads something is wrong with me. For me it was the total opposite, this diagnosis was a big relief. For the first time in my life, I felt like I was not just a dumb kid who was incapable of learning. There was some sort of an answer, a plan, something that could help me be who I wanted to be this whole time, normal.

My issues didn't melt away after my diagnosis, it was definitely a process. They prescribed Ritalin. A dose for the day and another dose for the evening doing my homework. Along with my new medication, they moved me to a special education stream where I was taking a course called Learning Strategies. I was not very happy to be taking that course but it was a better alternative than going to a BTI. While in my Learning Strategies class I really excelled, I was learning how to organize myself, study habits and how to write an essay. I really took school seriously and really worked to get myself back on track. I was not perfect but definitely I focused on getting out of special education and back into the mainstream. By eleventh grade, I was mostly caught up and taking advanced level courses, but I still had not recovered in regards to my self-esteem. Although my grades had improved, I still had no desire to go on to post-secondary.

A year later, I transferred to a new school and I struggled once again to fit in. I had some issues trying to find my social footing as well as continue some of the good habits that I had learned in Learning Strategies. I was committed to finishing high school and did successfully. With the uncertainty of what was next I didn't want to cross the stage and accept my diploma but I did for all the commitment my mother had put into getting me to this point. Still, I had zero interest in going to post-secondary. My mother had always planned for me to go to college or university and I'm sure it came as a shock to her when I showed no inclination of going. My mother is a very high achieving woman and when she is ready, she is very strong willed to put it nicely. She had a rule in our house that, if you aren't in school you are working. So that's what I did, I went out into the work world straight out of high school. At first, I went and did security and even contemplated becoming a police officer. My strong willed mother never giving up on the idea of me going to college or university drove me to investigate education. I looked into courses to take just to appease her and applied to a few schools to take up journalism, entertainment management and creative advertising. My heart was not in any of those courses but people around me tried to help guide me in courses they thought I'd find interesting. I didn't get accepted into any of those courses, so I continued to work. At this time, I was working two jobs.

One in security and the other at an electronic retail store. While working I determined that I had to grow up a lot and learned about accountability, taking care of my own responsibilities and keeping myself organized. I still wasn't ready to go to school, I had no plan.

While working at the electronic store I met this guy Kevin, he and I had a similar history in terms of our educational experience. We went out to grab a bite after work one day and just started talking about life and growing up. He told me horror stories about his journey through the educational system and that he went to a BTI. I was shocked. All I could think was, how did this guy just admit that he was a BTI kid. He didn't seem like a dumb guy, he didn't seem like a troublemaker or someone with no future. He didn't have the same stigma I had attached to a BTI kid. He had even been told some discouraging words from a teacher who told him to forget going to college because people from his school and background didn't make it. Something inside of him would not accept it. He told me that he was attending college in the fall, wasn't sure what he wanted to take but he would figure that out along the way. After that first conversation, we hit it off and would spend time talking and joking around. He would often encourage me to take another look at education. Every opportunity he had he would drop it in the conversation. It was different coming from a friend and I did not perceive it as nagging but as encouragement. One day he came into work and gave me a college program book and told me to read through it. I spent time looking at the different programs trying to find out something that I could do and would be good at. I came to a program and as soon as I read it, I knew it was for me.

I enrolled in the Child and Youth program as a mature student at a few colleges. I got accepted to one close to home and was starting in September. Leading up to the start of the program I was so nervous, all the doubts about myself started to creep back in. I looked at the other students and wondered if I was the oldest in the room, will they judge me? Will I be able to do the work? My friend, now my best friend Kevin was starting his second program and he came to check on me my first day. We talked a few minutes before my day started and he decided to switch his program on the spot to my program. We ended up in all the same classes in the first year. For some people having your best friend in your classes could be a disaster, especially for someone like me who was easily distracted and impulsive. It was the total opposite. Having Kevin with me was one of the best things that could have ever happened. We worked well together, bouncing ideas off each other; we would always study together for tests and exams and work on projects together. For the first time I felt excited about school and getting my tests back. We often would compete for the highest grade between not only us but also the whole class. Something had changed. I had grown somehow. I was in full blossom learning for the first time that I really and truly had all the abilities. I believed that I was smart and that no course would be able to stop me. I remembered all the days of despair and stress I had about learning and how I would shrink at the mere thought of school. I was flying; I went through college proving that I could make it, knowing I would move on and be successful.

I graduated and finished near the top of my class proudly walking away with more than my diploma but also knowing that I was able to overcome all obstacles put in front of me.

I was proud that I could walk across the stage in front of my mother who never gave up on me. I was proud that I could walk across the stage in front of my niece and nephew and be an example for them to see. I was most proud that I could walk across the stage as a kid who once spent too much time in the office.

My issues with Attention Deficit Hyperactive Disorder did not fly away, every day I battle with that label and how it affects my life. Sometimes I become distracted and have trouble finishing tasks. Sometimes my own doubts creep in when I am trying to make decisions and sometimes I feel insecure. Now as a father, I fear that my son could have inherited the same traits. Writing this story and remembering my journey assures me and helps me put that all to rest. All that I have gone through has equipped me to deal with doubts and fears because I know what to do. I now work in the school board with students in the special education system. I sometimes see them shrink and deflate, feeling like they have no options and are disenfranchised from the education system; and I see myself. I often think about what would I have needed to make it through those days and I try to be what I didn't have.

My label does not define me. Your label may not be ADHD, or BTI Kid but whatever the label, you never let it define where you are going or who you are.

PRINCIPLES FROM NICHOLAS' STORY

PRINCIPLE 1:
Labels Are Just Words But Not Definitions Of Who You Really Are

The label of mental health has so many stigmas attached to it. Many of the thoughts connected to mental health are negative. Don't allow people or societal norms tell you who you are. I once heard a poet say, "Be the author of your own horoscope." It has always stuck with me. I won't allow someone to tell me how my day will be or how I will be. I would far rather decide that for myself.

PRINCIPLE 2:
A Diagnosis Can Be A Positive Thing; It Gave Me Options And Perspective

This can be a hard one to digest. Diagnoses are hard things to accept, some can be much more life altering than the one I received. I don't make light of how painful and hard they may be on families, but they definitely give perspective and give another lens to look through in life. I was able to accept my diagnosis and it helped me see myself differently.

PRINCIPLE 3:

Having The Right Support System Helps

I was lucky to find my best friend Kevin at the time I did. He helped me so much in this season of my life. He pushed me to keep going and to get to where I needed to be. It's important that we surround ourselves with people that have our best interests at heart.

PRINCIPLE 4:

Doubts and Fears Don't Go Away

Our perceptions of the challenge changes as we meet and defeat them. When I entered that classroom, I was afraid that despite how far I have come I might fail again. However, I was able to draw from the small successes that I had along the way to help me. Those successes added up, my confidence grew and fear dissipated. I didn't even look at school as a challenge of my ability anymore.

PRINCIPLE 5:

Parents Should Not Be Afraid To Look For Answers

If you are concerned about the mental health of your children, you should not be afraid of looking for answers from professionals. Medication may not be the answer; the answer could be something else. You will not know until you investigate. When in doubt get a second opinion.

NICHOLAS BARHAM

Nicholas continues to give back to the community through his efforts with Brothers from the 6, a community based organization created to empower and support the lives of youth in Toronto and the Greater Toronto Area. He currently works for the York Region District School Board as a Child and Youth Worker and volunteers as an assistant basketball coach, striving to be the support to students he works with that he needed as a student. Nicholas currently resides in Whitby Ontario with his wife and young King Bryce.

CHAPTER TEN

MY STORY IS NOT FOR EVERYBODY
BY CHRIS DUFF

"Growth is painful. Change is painful. But nothing is as painful as staying stuck somewhere you don't belong."
Mandy Hale

My story is not for everybody.

My story is not for the person who has everything figured out. It is not meant for the person that knows what they want in life and is pursuing it daily. My story is not meant for the person that feels there is nothing wrong with the current system we live in. My story is not meant for the person that is satisfied with settling for a life of mediocrity. I'm sharing my story for the person that is stuck, frustrated and dissatisfied with where they are in life and confused about the direction they want to go. It is for the person that is unclear about their purpose, passion and potential.

My story is for the person that believes deep down they were never put on this planet to just work, pay bills and die. My story is for the person that is ready to UNLEARN. Unlearn the system. Unlearn "you" and unlearn what we've defined to be life. For some of you, my story will put into words what you've been struggling with for some time. A feeling that you are not lazy. You are not complacent. There is nothing wrong with you. You are just stuck. You're stuck between a place of desiring more out of life and the reality of a system that has been carefully crafted to only give you the status quo.

What's worse is that so many of us have become masters at creating this illusion that we're, "Living our best life," but deep down, we're lost and confused. To add to the complexity, on paper it would appear that many of us have everything figured out. I'm checking off the boxes on this laundry list of things to do on my "adulting" checklist. I have my degree. Check. I'm working in my field. Check. I've got the car. Check. I'm working towards the property. Check. I'm doing everything I was supposed to do, yet, I still feel unsatisfied. I still feel unfulfilled.

Over the next several pages, I lay out a blueprint that will help you to become unstuck. It will help you understand the stage of life you're in, more importantly, provide you with the knowledge and tools you need to navigate through that stage. To help provide context, peppered throughout this passage, I share my own personal experience of how I leveraged this breakthrough process to discover an alternative way of living and succeeding in life. What I am proposing is that for you to become unstuck, it requires more than a change in your behaviour or a few motivational posts on social media. It requires a transformation of your mindset.

It requires an unlearning of the years of conditioning you've undergone. Over the next several pages, I lay out a framework that I have used and that I continue to use to teach others how to achieve this shift. I've divided the process into four distinct stages.

1. **The Conflict**
2. **The Discovery**
3. **The Unlearning**
4. **The Conquest**

It is worth noting that this process may not always be linear, but more often than not, your journey to your breakthrough will include each of these stages.

Let's get into this.

The Conflict

*"Identity cannot be found or fabricated but emerges
from within when one has the courage to let go."*
Doug Cooper

The first stage of the process is The Conflict Stage. It is a stage that is characterized by a belief that; I am not who my past experiences are trying to tell me to be. I am not who my parents say I am. I am not who society says I am. I am not who my friends say I am. I am who I say I am and I will become who I say I want to become. It is this single belief that gives birth to your conflict. The next logical question is, what is this a conflict between? The conflict is between external belief systems superimposed upon your internal belief system. What often happens is, we form a belief system and an identity using external influences such as belief systems from your parents, friends, society and experiences. So, if I have no conflict when my parents tell me I should be a doctor or an engineer, I blindly accept that identity and pursue that career. If I had been cheated on and abused in past relationships, I allow those experiences to turn me into a person filled with bitterness and malice. However, for those of you in this stage, you're here because deep down in the crevices of your soul, there is a version of you saying, this is not who I am, and this is the point of tension.

To look at this another way, I want to use an analogy. The story of the mass suicides at the Igbo Landing. The Igbo Landing is a historic site at Dunbar Creek on St. Simons Island, Glynn County, Georgia. In 1803, a captive group of Igbo people, an ethnic group native to what we call Nigeria today, had taken control of their slave ship because they refused to become slaves in America. It is said that in an act of resistance, they drowned their captors and then at the direction of their high chief, they walked into the marshy waters of Dunbar Creek, committing mass suicide. Here's the thing; if the Igbo people ascribed to the belief system of their captors, there would have been no revolt. There would have been no push back. There ultimately would have been no conflict. They would have believed their worth stopped at the $100 they were purchased for. The conflict arose because they NEVER ascribed to the idea that they were meant to be slaves. They never ascribed to the idea that they were meant to live in captivity. Therefore, the conflict stage in the process is imperative because it signifies that you are still in the fight. It signifies that there is still a level of discomfort with who you are.

However, if you're in this period of contention, I need you to understand that you are right where you need to be, because The Conflict Stage sets the entire breakthrough process in motion. If there were no conflict, there would be no indication of the need for change. Here's what I mean. Figuratively speaking, I believe that people are pregnant. We are pregnant with a purpose. We are all put on this planet to accomplish something. I truly believe that. As we live our lives, we are either killing or feeding this purpose growing inside of us. For many of you, during this conflicting period, your purpose is kicking and it's kicking to tell you you're not where you are supposed to be.

Let's look at this another way. One of the reasons a baby will kick or move during a pregnancy is because they are uncomfortable with the position their mother is in. Reread that, because I think you just missed it. One of the reasons you can feel that thing inside of you kicking, one of the reasons you are in your conflict stage is because your purpose is uncomfortable with the position you are in. It is uncomfortable with you waking up, going to work, coming home and having contributed nothing to this world. It is uncomfortable with you settling for a life of mediocrity. It is uncomfortable with you checking off the boxes on your "adulting" grocery list when you are really not satisfied. It is uncomfortable with you settling into a life that was never meant for you. So, it kicks and kicks and kicks and kicks, until one day it stops. If you're in the medical field (or simply have access to a search engine) you'll know that if a baby stops kicking, after a certain period of gestation or if there is no or reduced fetal movement, this can be a sign of fetal distress. This could be a sign that your baby is dead and for some of you, this is exactly where you are. With each day that passes, you feel less kicks and less nudges. Until one day it stops. So understand that if there's a conflict, it is a good thing, because it indicates there are still signs of life.

As far back as I can remember I had always resided in my own bubble. I rarely tried new things. I lived within my comfort zone. I was very introverted. Very reserved. Shy. Socially awkward. In the same breath, as far back as I can remember, I always struggled with feelings of not belonging. Feelings of being different and just always struggling to fit in. I would argue that the person that I had become wasn't me. In a way, I had formulated this identity because of influences from my family, traumatic experiences from my childhood, experiences at church, relationships with friends and experiences at school. In my adolescent years, this identity was manageable but because I had let feelings, pain and hurt fester. In my teen years, the crisis became more complex. These experiences coupled with pain eventually gave birth to a myriad of mental health challenges.

This is where the plot thickens.

When you compound unresolved pain from childhood experiences with experiences of physical abuse, low self-esteem and feelings of hopelessness, you get a special cocktail of things spiraling out of control. An example of this was when I decided to drop out of high school in my last year. Looking back I realized that this had very little to do with school itself and everything to do with the struggle with my mental health. This wasn't spoken about in the community that I was from but that didn't make me immune to the tribulation. I struggled with my confidence. I struggled with my self-esteem. Every comment, whether a joke or insult, seemed to pierce through my self-esteem like a sharp dart through flesh and it was largely because I was in such a fragile state. But again, this wasn't me. Until I started believing that it was. I had gotten to such a dark place. I felt that I couldn't do it anymore. I couldn't endure the pain. It was unbearable. If that wasn't enough, I had lost hope that it would ever get better. I remember the next few moments almost moving in slow motion. I was in the basement watching TV and tears began streaming down my cheek. I remember walking up the three flights of stairs hearing the creak, as each stair responded to the weight of each step. After what seemed like eternity, I made my way into my parent's room and into their bathroom where I found my mother's blue basket. I remember my movements being almost zombie-like. No emotion. Blank stares. No more tears. I had made my decision. I grabbed a bottle of pills. I exited the room and walked back down to the garage. I remember having to step over a bike, some boxes and other items that filled our garage at the time. I sat down on the floor. The very cold and very dirty floor. I sat there. I remember glancing over at a red toolbox and memories of me fixing bikes when I was young flashed into my mind. My left hand firmly gripped the small bottle as my right hand worked to open the lid. For some reason I struggled. I don't know if it was because my hands were shaking or if it was the safety cap. I just remember it taking longer than it should have. Once I got it open, I raised it to my lips and poured several into my mouth. I just remember chewing. I don't remember thinking or feeling anything. I just remember sitting there. Staring blankly and then I must have knocked out. When I woke up, I was on the garage floor. I was disoriented and discombobulated. For a moment, I didn't know where I was and what happened. When I came too, I realized my attempt was unsuccessful. I cried. I just sat there full of feelings of mixed emotions. I sat there for about an hour just in my thoughts. My mind racing. Negative thoughts. Positive thoughts. An array of emotions. Anger. Sadness. Confusion. I decided to get up. Struggling with balance, I went inside the house, grabbed my Discman and went for a walk. I thought it was a CD with music, but it turned out to be a sermon by Bishop TD Jakes called "See Your Way Clear". This sermon was transformational for me because it validated what I had been feeling over the years. It helped me realize that the very differences that I always saw as negatives were actually positives. This message empowered me to seek help. With absolutely no exaggeration, this sermon saved my life and that was not by accident.

Over the next few years, unbeknownst to him, Bishop Jakes became my therapist. I would listen to his sermons every day. I would listen to them at work, at home, at the gym, whenever and wherever. I would fill my mind with his insight and his inspiration. It put so much of what I was going through into perspective. He helped me to articulate the pain. The anger. The range of emotion. Everything. I remember in one of his sermons he said, "Never put a period where there should only be a comma." This one hit me like a sack of bricks, because it was exactly what I attempted to do when I tried to take my life. I was trying to end my life during a period that would eventually pass. Bishop TD Jakes started me on my journey to healing and this became one of the key phases that would eventually change the entire trajectory of my life forever. What he did was arm me with the validation and inspiration I needed to believe that I was right. I am not who "they" said I was. I'm fearfully and wonderfully made. I am a conqueror. I'm made in the image of God. I am powerful. I did not have to become the person my experiences were trying to make me become. This was exactly what I needed to hear, someone reaffirming what I had felt. For most of you, this is the message that you need. Once you have this validation and affirmation, the question becomes, how do I transition out of this conflict stage? Simple. Begin to act on the mustard seed of belief that you are not who they say you are. Begin to act on the belief that there is a version of you, deep down, that is yet to be explored, experienced and nurtured. In The Discovery Stage, we examine further, what actions need to be taken to transition out of your conflict.

The Discovery

"I am not a product of my circumstances. I am a product of my decisions."
Stephen Covey

The Discovery Stage begins when your question of, "Who Am I?" meets action. It is a stage where, not only do you believe that there's an alternative version of you, but you set yourself on a journey to discover and further explore that version of yourself. This stage is not just for the person who is ready to reflect on the question of, "Who Am I?" It's for the person who is ready to act on the question, because The Discovery Stage is about learning through experience, not just learning theoretically. As amazing as I believe this book you are reading is, the reality is, you will only discover a fraction of who you are if your efforts do not extend beyond what you read here. This is because there are certain parts of who you are that can only be discovered through experience.

When I work with people to help them kick-start their journey of self-discovery, I get them to do two things; first, recognize that they will never discover who they are through theory. You can read all of the books, listen to the greatest podcasts, but until you get out there and try things- you will never learn who you are. The second is that I bring them through a process that I call the 3E's. Expose, Explore and Experiment.

If you are looking to discover you, you need to Expose yourself to new learning, new experiences, new ideas and new opportunities.

It is about being willing to be open to new learning. Stretching outside of your comfort zone. Stepping into unfamiliar territory. For me, I had two key moments where exposure really changed the course of my life. The first one was when I ventured to open my first business. Exposure to business completely changed my perspective. It helped me to discover my capabilities. With entrepreneurship, there was no box I was put in. I could be as creative as I wanted. There was an element of freedom. Freedom to create. Freedom to build. Freedom to experiment. Freedom to use my mind. This helped me to realize that I was so much more than manual labour. I was creative.

The second experience was my mission trip to India. This trip exposed me to life outside of the life I was living. It showed me poverty. In many ways, this trip changed my perspective on life. I knew I was passionate about business, but I had always thought I was going to use the principles of business to get the bag and make money moves. What my India experience revealed to me was that I wanted to use these principles of business to affect and create change in neglected and forgotten parts of the world. I wanted to use business to improve the lives of those around me. Fast forward to today, this is exactly what I am blessed with the opportunity to do. Through one of my companies, we support young leaders who are passionate about creating change. We help them to develop businesses that are solving real-world problems. Why? Because we know we cannot change the world by ourselves. For us to reach our goal of impacting billions of people around the world, we need to empower leaders with the support they need to change their local communities. We've since opened branches in The Philippines and Uganda and are laying the groundwork for Pakistan.

The second E stands for Explore. This is about diving deeper into what piqued your interest in the previous stage. This is where you focus on learning more. You dive deeper into the theoretical side of what piqued your interest. Get curious. Ask questions. You can read books, listen to podcasts, watch videos or read articles. You just want to work towards learning as much as you can about that given topic. For myself, when business became an interest to me, I began to read articles, watched CNBC and other business networks, watched videos, went to workshops and seminars, switched my major to business and much more. This stage is about theoretical discovery.

The last E is for Experiment. This is about taking action by using the information that you've been learning in the Explore stage, putting it to work and making it practical. There is always a learning curve between theory and practice, but when you experiment, you begin to close that gap. How? Because experimentation cannot happen theoretically, action has to be taken. For myself, much of what I was learning I was applying to the business in real time, but I also learned a number of things about myself. For example, I saw how I responded when I had gotten in difficult situations. I discovered how much I hated cold calling and how I responded to rejection. For you, this experimentation may take the form of starting a podcast. It may look like volunteering. It may look like creating a side hustle. It may be launching a YouTube series. It may look like you starting a blog site. Regardless of what it is that you do, the point is you do something.

At this point in my journey, it had been validated that I was not who society said I was. I was wonderfully made. I was awesome! My past experiences didn't define me. Public opinions no longer carried any weight. I felt like a new me. The challenge was I still never knew who I was. Once I realized that there was a version of myself buried deep under all of these experiences and the manufactured identity I commenced my new journey to discovering me. Discovering what I was capable of. What I could really accomplish. Discover my passion and realize my purpose on this planet.

While attending York University, I worked for a cleaning company making $10/hour. We would clean restaurants such as Montana's, Applebee's and others. After 3 months, I passed my probation and my boss had approached me with a proposition to either receive a $3 raise or open up a business, become a subcontractor and make triple what I brought in as an employee. However, at this point I had no interest in business and zero interest in running my own company. So I opted out and decided to take the raise. That night, I spent some time thinking about it. I was 21, still living at home, what did I have to lose? So, I registered the business. I called up a friend and we opened "One of A Kind Cleaning Services". My first ever business venture. This decision was an extremely pivotal and transformative one for me. They say there are a few defining moments in a person's life. Well, this was one of mine. It was defining because it allowed me to see the benefits of stepping outside of what was familiar, venturing into the unknown and exploring the benefits found on the other side.

I wanted my business to grow. I went to workshops and programs run by the city and community organizations. The deeper I dove into the world of business, the more I fell in love with it. Reading papers, researching and watching business news on CNBC and BNN. My entire life was about business. Around this same time, I went to India on a mission trip. This trip exposed me to life outside of the life I was living. It showed me poverty. In many ways, this trip changed my perspective on life. I had seen human beings eating out of the same mountains of garbage as animals. I saw entire families living on the street (newborns, kids, parents and grandparents). I saw families sitting outside of apartments while the mother was inside selling her body to a john for money to feed her family. It opened my eyes to problems of humanity. Problems, which I realized I wanted to fix.

What my India experience gave me was direction. I was passionate about business, because I loved the principles and the strategy, but my experience in India gave me a place to channel my passion for business. I wanted to do good with it. This was another slice of insight into who I really was.

Fast forward a few years, I decided to try for a job at McDonald's. The reason is that McDonald's trains you to manage a multimillion-dollar company. They teach you about systems, accounting, labour management, inventory management and much more. I wanted hands-on training and I saw this as an opportunity to get paid to learn. After three months, I moved from being a manager-in-training to an assistant manager. Fast forward a few more years, my true colours began to show in this company. I would create initiatives within the restaurant such as a Kings & Queens Appreciation Event where we would treat all staff like royalty for an entire week. We would give gifts, coupons and some good TLC. This experience gave me a slice of insight into who I really was. It showed me how much I loved developing people, investing in them and having a hand in their transformation.

As I began to launch innovative and creative projects in the restaurant, I began to realize the type of ceiling I was hitting. I was only allowed to be so creative, but I wanted room to unleash my wings. I wanted to continue developing initiatives for the restaurant. I quickly came to realize that at McDonald's; I became what botanist call a root bound plant. A plant becomes root bound when the roots begin to outgrow the environment it is in, as a result, it restricts how high the plant grows and I wanted to grow. The challenge was the environment I was in restricted me. I decided to take it outside of McDonald's. On the weekends, I would host workshops where I would invite the young staff from my restaurant and teach them about financial literacy, passion, vision and life skills (the subjects that you don't learn in school). This gave me another slice of insight into my identity. It made me realize that I loved empowering and educating people. Especially young people. On June 23rd, 2013, I hosted my first workshop and I entered into a new phase in my life.

The Discovery Stage will give you what I call DNA or slices of insight that will help reveal to you the version of yourself buried underneath the rubble. It will reveal to you, the things that truly bring you joy. It will show you the person you are, as well as the person you want to become. One of the most crucial steps in The Discovery Stage is to use the experiences, along with introspective insights you collect and create a new identity. If you believe you are in this stage, I encourage you to journal your new experiences. What did you enjoy? What did you not enjoy? What about these activities invigorates you? What makes you come alive? Is there anything specific that you learned about yourself during these experiences? What role(s) did you naturally gravitate towards? This will help you form your new persona. It is with this new persona that you enter into your Unlearning stage.

THE UNLEARNING

"We are going to emancipate ourselves from mental slavery because whilst others might free the body, none but ourselves can free the mind."

MARCUS GARVEY

In my mid-20's, I began to realize something about the world we were living in. We were manufactured. What we valued. What we were working towards. Who we were and who we were striving to be. For many of us, who we were was often a result of the conditioning and cultivating of the system we were living in. I began to recognize that the system I was living in, didn't care about my purpose and it didn't care about my passion. The system I was living in wasn't concerned about what I was put on this earth to accomplish. They system was concerned with one thing and one thing only; maximize profit.

The intricate fabric of society was built around this philosophy. When I went to school to pursue my education; bachelors, masters or PhD, I thought it was about me, but it wasn't. It was about maximizing profit. If I had graduated and began, so earnestly, searching for that job; 70k a year plus benefits, I would have thought it was about me, but it wouldn't have been. It is about maximizing profit. The system was not designed to help you discover who you were called to be. The system was designed to help you become a cog that fits into someone else's machine. In the process of this, we lose the very essence of who we are at our core. Have you ever wondered how generations upon generations of people have been convinced that it is more important for them to know about Shakespeare, Western Civilization, Physics, Algebra, Biology and Calculus than it is for them to know about who they are at their core? Their passion? Their purpose on this earth? The answer is conditioning. Have you ever wondered how you could convince people that their life will begin at 65 (or retirement), when life expectancy in Canada is around 80? The answer is conditioning. Have you ever wondered how you could get generations to believe they are only as valuable as the skills an employer will hire them for? The answer is conditioning. Have you ever wondered how you could get people to believe that their sole purpose on this planet is to work, pay bills and die? The answer is conditioning.

Let's take a deeper look.

I work with youth on a day-to-day basis. I work with them in schools, in the community, detention centers and more. In my conversations with them, I often ask them one question- what do you want to do with your life? I will often get two answers; I don't know or they list a career. Not knowing what they want to do doesn't bother me, but when they share a career, I'm disturbed. Here's why. As simple as it may seem, what they are doing in that moment is defining their future as work and the biggest challenge with this is that they begin to see their career as their life's destination. So, in their mind, everything that I am doing now, all of the decisions that I am making today is so that I can get a job and more importantly, a job in my field. What no one tells me is that once I get a job in my field, after a few decades, I begin to look forward to retirement. In all honesty, is this really what life is? It can't be. When I deliver our Passioneering workshop, I encourage young people to consider finding a way to use their career as leverage to build the life that they want. When you see your career as your life's destination, you end up falling into the rattrap. You wake up, you go to work, you come home and sleep. That's Monday. Tuesday, you wake up, go to work, come home and sleep. Wednesday, you wake up, you go to work, you come home and sleep. Thursday, same thing. Friday, however, is a little different. You wake up, go to work, come home, get ready, go out, turn up and then come home. Saturday, you chill or socialize. Sunday, you chill and socialize and repeat the same cycle over in the next week. You live to work, pay bills and die.

Another reason why an answer of their career concerns me is that in the large scheme of things, they'll spend about 25% of their life actually working, but they've defined their future as work. Let's look at this another way. When I ask a young person, what do you want to do with your life, what I'm asking them is, "What do you want to do with the 8,760 hours you've been given in any particular year?" (You get that number when you multiply 24 hours per day x 365 days per year). When they tell me a career, they're referring to the 2,080 hours that they will spend working. (You get this number when you multiply 40 hours per week (average) x 52 weeks per year). The difference between the 8,760 (hours that you have to live) and the 2,080 (hours you will work) is 6,680 hours. 6,680 hours that often go unaccounted for. 6,680 hours that no one really thinks about how to maximize. That's 400,800 minutes and 24,048,000 seconds. Furthermore, I am not saying that this unaccounted for time is not being utilized. I am merely proposing that this unaccounted for time is not being maximized. Our entire focus is often fixated on the 2,080 hours that we will spend working in our career. So no wonder we easily fall into the rattrap of working to pay bills and then dying. A mindset carefully constructed and cultivated from when we were young. The question is, from where? Let's explore this further.

When you get into junior kindergarten, let's count that as year one. Fast forward to when you graduate Grade 12. You would have spent 14 years of your life in school and not just any years; these are your most critical years. The years of your life where you are most impressionable. Now, let's say you were to go on and graduate after four years of post-secondary. This would have now been 18 years of your life in school. My question for you is simple; which number from our equation is school preparing you for?

Hours to Live: 8,760

Hours to Work: 2,080

Difference: 6,680

If you answered 2,080 hours, you are absolutely correct! School is designed to prepare you for the workforce. It is designed to prepare you for the 2,080 hours. Therefore, we essentially spend 18 years of our life preparing for the 2,080 hours per year that we will be working. WOW! So no wonder the entire 24 hours of our day revolve around the 8 hours that I'm at work. No wonder I believe it's more important for me to know about Western Civilization, parabolic functions, trigonometry, photosynthesis than it is to know about me and everything that makes me, me. No wonder so many of us feel empty, purposeless and that our lives are meaningless. We have been groomed to become something that we were never designed to be – a worker. We were always meant to use work as a tool to achieve something greater. I do not believe we were ever meant to just work.

To further this point, if school teaches me how to maximize the 2,080 hours I'll be working, what teaches me to maximize the remaining 6,680 hours? To my knowledge there is no institution, framework, ecosystem or infrastructure set up to teach people how to discover themselves. This is the reason we are in the predicament we are in.

Discovering you takes unlearning who you are told to be and this is challenging because it requires you to go against much of what you know. It may even require you to go against the ideas, values and beliefs of many people in your life because this mindset has been ingrained into our very outlook on life. We need to go through this process of unlearning and give ourselves the ability to choose an alternative to the way we are currently living life.

THE CONQUEST

"Where your talents and a need in the world cross,
there lies your vocation."
Aristotle

As I am in The Conquest Stage, I am on a mission and the best way for me to describe my mission is to draw a correlation to Marvel's X-Men. X-Men were considered mutants because their abilities were positioned outside of the colouring lines of societal norms. They possessed superhuman abilities. They were different. A difference that society led them to believe was an abnormality. A difference that society purported was dangerous. A difference that society convinced them to believe was a deficiency. However, unbeknownst to them, this abnormality was their gift-wrapped aptitude in seed form. What they desperately needed was a cultivator. In walks Professor X, the founder and leader of the X-Men. What was most profound to me was not his telepathic ability, his scientific genius or that he was an authority in genetics. What was most profound to me was his desire to shelter and train mutants from around the world through The Xavier Institute for Higher Learning. An academy that taught mutants to control and explore their powers. He taught them to use their gifts as a force for good and not evil. He peeled back the layers of conditioning and misinformation that declared something was wrong with them. He helped them to discover their true identity; who they were, what they were capable of and what they offered the world. He provided them with the validation, inspiration and preparation that helped them navigate through their conflict stage. This work of Professor X encapsulates my mission.

Figuratively, I believe that people are like X-Men, minus the costumes and the superpowers. When you look at X-Men there are three things you cannot deny. Their uniqueness, their diversity and their gifts. To me, this embodies humanity in our quintessential form. We are gushing with this uncanny uniqueness and for many of us, buried underneath the rubble of conditioning and misinformation, we have seeds of gifts, skills and talents that, if nurtured could change the world. This is what I have dedicated my life to doing; helping people re-explore and re-discover themselves. Today, through my portfolio of companies, we are working to help people peel back the layers of conditioning and reset their factory settings. Helping them re-explore, re-discover and reinvent themselves.

The Conquest Stage in the journey is about action and purpose. It is a moment in time where you understand who you truly are, what you offer this world and you find opportunities to use it. It is about your contribution to the world through your work. A period where your passion and your gifts, meet the world's deepest needs. In this stage of the process, work is redefined and the value it provides transcends extrinsic motivators, such as money or accolades. Rather, the value is to be found in things that are intrinsic. It is the work itself that begins to motivate you. Your life's purpose becomes clearer and you begin to live your life through a singular mission. In this stage, work becomes an extension of your core identity.

THE CONCLUSION

"The difference between who you are and who you want to be is what you do."
- Unknown -

My intention with this passage was never to change your life. My hope was that it would plant a seed. A seed that served a dual purpose. On one side, I wanted this seed to challenge you. Challenge what you've been taught as truth. Challenge your definition of life and challenge who you've defined yourself to be. On the other hand, I want this seed to act as a catalyst. A catalyst that helps you pursue the life you were designed to live. A catalyst that sparks a conversation. My hope is that no matter what you do after reading this passage, you never look at life the same again.

PRINCIPLES FROM CHRIS' STORY

PRINCIPLE 1:

Becoming Unstuck Requires A Shift In Your Mindset

Becoming unstuck requires more than posting inspirational and motivational content on social media or embarking on a 30-day challenge. It requires a shift in your mindset. It requires a conscious and cognizant decision not just stating that you want to change, but that you WILL change. From here, you begin to develop the habits and behaviours needed to sustain the change.

PRINCIPLE 2:

Discovery of Self Must Be Introspective & Experiential

You will never discover who you truly are and what you are truly capable of by only reading personal development books, listening to podcasts or going to personal development seminars. Discovering you requires Exposure, Exploration and Experimentation. Exposure representing your decision to step outside of your comfort zone and immerse yourself into new ventures, new territories and new arenas. Then further identifying specific areas that you find interesting. Exploration representing the theoretical journey you will take to learn more about what emerged from exposing yourself to new things. Take courses. Read books. Listen to podcasts. Watch videos. Dedicate time to further explore the topic of interest. Lastly, Experimentation represents experiential learning. Take what you have been learning theoretically about the area of interest and apply it pragmatically. This could be through taking up a hobby, volunteering in the particular field of interest, starting a business, getting a new job or even interning. The idea here is to practically experiment with this new area of interest.

PRINCIPLE 3:

You Were Never Put On This Earth To Just Work, Pay Bills & Die

Recognize that who you have become has been manufactured meticulously by a system that wants you to value, pursue and attain specific things. However, buried deep down in the crevices of your soul is another version of you that wants to live. Rediscover who you were before the world told you who you should be. Find that thing that makes you come alive, because that is what the world desperately needs. People who have found what makes them come alive.

PRINCIPLE 4:

The Difference Between Who You Are And Who You Want To Be Is What You Do

Many of us will attest to the idea that we are striving professionally towards greater accomplishments. A doctorate degree, a higher position at our jobs or even financial goals. The problem is, too many of us fail to carry the same ambition when it comes to our personal lives. In fact, our personal lives are often set to autopilot. What would happen if we carried that same level of intensity that we have for our professional lives into our personal lives? Who would we become if we put just as much effort into becoming our best selves as we put into becoming the best employee? Take time and journal the person you are today. Then journal your blueprint - who do you want to become? Ask yourself, what do I need to do to become this person? What courses do I need to take? What skills do I need to develop? What characteristics do I need to work on? Then go do it. It's just that simple.

CHRIS DUFF

Christopher Duff is a speaker, entrepreneur and youth advocate fiercely committed to helping young people thrive in life and become the best version of themselves. He is the founder and president of Inspired Initiatives Inc. - a grassroots youth development firm that works to help young people develop the skills, knowledge and competencies needed to thrive in the 21st Century. Through his work, he has inspired tens of thousands of youth globally and works with the top school boards across Canada. He is also the co-founder of The Brilliance Academy, which is a social enterprise on a mission to change the face of education by making school a place to discover your true identity, explore your human potential and illuminate your genius within.

You Have the Keys Now Drive:
5 Keys and 5 Habits to Personal Change

Author and Coach Danny Stone shares 5 keys and 5 habits to personal change. In You Have the Keys, Now Drive he helps you master your mindset and take control of your life. As an expert in transformation, Danny Stone provides you with a step-by-step program teaching you essential habits to change your mindset, conquer

YouHaveTheKeysNowDrive.com

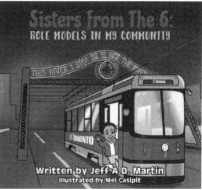

"Brothers from the 6/ Sister from the 6: Role models in my Community"

2 in 1 Children's book, was created by Jeff A.D. Martin to inspire children at a younger age to strive for greatness. To recognize that there are people who are from similar neighborhoods, upbringings and backgrounds who had found success and to show a representation of role models; a mirrored reflection of what they can look like when they grow up.

Also available at InspireLegacyCompany.com

Also, listen to Motivating from the 6. The podcast that motivates you to step into your greatness and find your true purpose. Listen in as Jeff brings you interviews from people who are smashing their industry, guests who will help you through your own difficulties and topics that are going to help you to become your best self. Listen in on Google Play, iTunes, Spreaker, TuneIn and everywhere podcasts are found.

The King of Quotes and Forward March books quote books are the kind of books that are meant to be kept close by because they are both inspiring and motivating. A quote or two a day by Jelani Daniel will remind you that the sky is the limit and you are more important than you think.

Also listen to the **King of Quotes Podcast** wherever podcasts can be found.

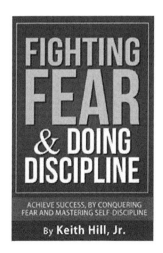

Fighting Fear & Doing Discipline: Achieve success, by conquering fear and mastering self-discipline

Fighting Fear and Doing Discipline will motivate you from behind the fears that hold you back from your goals and dreams. It will then teach you how to maintain and grow your success through self-discipline. Keith Hill, Jr.'s style is both comedic and knowledgeable, and it allows for an entertaining and informative read. With age-old wisdom and personal insight, "Fight and Do" can speak to the book-smart and the street-smart person alike; it is useful for everyone from young students to seasoned entrepreneurs.

keithhilljr.com

With an unflinching eye, an extraordinary ear, and a story as timely as any on the nightly news, poet Randell Adjei brings us **I AM NOT MY STRUGGLES,** a collection of poetry so honest and beautiful you won't want to put it down. Randell Adjei's is a story of a reckless youth, early incarceration and the lessons learned, and, above all, resilience. Randell Adjei writes to know himself and to redeem himself, as well as to honor his mother, her homeland, and all the young people who come after him. The energy in **I AM NOT MY STRUGGLES** in infectious; once you begin the first poem you'll find yourself rapt until the very last word of the book.

randelladjei.com

Follow the movement:

FACEBOOK: KNew Me Movement

INSTAGRAM: @knew.me.movement

Printed in Great Britain
by Amazon

35373395R00137